MELTDOWN ON MAIN STREET

MELTDOWN
ON
MAIN STREET

❖

WHY SMALL BUSINESS
IS LEADING THE REVOLUTION
AGAINST BIG GOVERNMENT

❖

Richard Lesher

With a Foreword by Newt Gingrich

A DUTTON BOOK

DUTTON
Published by the Penguin Group
Penguin Books USA Inc., 375 Hudson Street,
New York, New York 10014, U.S.A.
Penguin Books Ltd, 27 Wrights Lane,
London W8 5TZ, England
Penguin Books Australia Ltd, Ringwood,
Victoria, Australia
Penguin Books Canada Ltd, 10 Alcorn Avenue,
Toronto, Ontario, Canada M4V 3B2
Penguin Books (N.Z.) Ltd, 182-190 Wairau Road,
Auckland 10, New Zealand

Penguin Books Ltd, Registered Offices:
Harmondsworth, Middlesex, England

First published by Dutton, an imprint of Dutton Signet,
a division of Penguin Books USA Inc.
Distributed in Canada by McClelland & Stewart Inc.

First Printing, May, 1996
10   9   8   7   6   5   4   3   2   1

REGISTERED TRADEMARK—MARCA REGISTRADA

Library of Congress Cataloging-in-Publication Data is available upon request.

Printed in the United States of America
Set in Simoncini Garamond
Designed by Stanley S. Drate/Folio Graphics Co., Inc.

This book is printed on acid-free paper.
⊗

To Agnes, my copilot,
with love

CONTENTS

ACKNOWLEDGMENTS   *ix*

FOREWORD BY NEWT GINGRICH   *xi*

PREFACE   *xvii*

1   A POLITICAL EARTHQUAKE   *1*

2   IN QUEST OF COMMON SENSE   *31*

3   SAVING THE ENVIRONMENT FROM
    ENVIRONMENTALISTS   *55*

4   LAYING DOWN THE LAW TO LAWYERS   *80*

5   DISCOURAGED EMPLOYERS   *101*

6   POVERTY AMERICAN STYLE   *132*

7   SPOTTED OWLS ARE RED HERRINGS   *152*

8 WHY GOVERNMENT IS THE PROBLEM 172

9 A VISION FOR THE MILLENNIUM 186

EPILOGUE 207

AUTHOR'S NOTE ON SOURCES 209

ACKNOWLEDGMENTS

I am profoundly grateful to many friends and associates who gave of their time and knowledge to help me develop this manuscript: Dr. Harvey Alter, who reviewed my analysis of environmental and natural resource issues; Peter Eide and Nancy Fulco, who critiqued my comments on labor law; Rae Nelson, who advised me on welfare reform and education; Dick Loomis, who arranged interviews with state and local chamber officials; Jeff Joseph, who advised on the scope and focus of this work; Lonnie Taylor and Jim Halloran, who rounded up the quotes and anecdotes from members of Congress; and Steve Bokat, who gave the entire opus a thorough legal review.

I offer special thanks to Hank Cox, who did the lion's share of research, writing, and editing for this project, and added more than a few insights of his own. Without Hank's superb writing skills, historical background, and thorough knowledge of the federal bureaucracy, this project would not have been possible.

FOREWORD
by Newt Gingrich

The title of this book, *Meltdown on Main Street,* summarizes what happened in the November 1994 elections, when the American people evicted the seemingly invincible Democratic majority that had ruled Congress and defined the national agenda virtually uninterrupted since the Korean War.

The upheaval clearly came as a shock to the major news media pundits, most of whom were predicting only modest Republican gains. A few of them thought it possible the Republicans could take control of the Senate temporarily, as they had when President Ronald Reagan swept into office in 1980, but that was as far as the establishment experts would go. The idea that the Republicans might also assume control of the House was simply not taken seriously.

Their skepticism was reasonable. After all, the Democrats had held the House in a death grip, controlling its powerful committees and vast budgetary power, since 1952, an unbroken forty-year run. Speakers of the House and chairmen of key committees came and went with some regularity, but the Democratic majority seemed as solid and unmovable as those implacable faces on Mount Rushmore.

Against that backdrop a growing number of voices were warning a major upheaval was coming. One of those voices was mine. Along with other members of the House minority leadership, I enjoyed direct access to our party's state and local organizations, which were following every Senate and House race closely. The numbers they were sending us were clear and unmistakable. We could hear the earth trembling beneath our feet. The long era of Democratic dominance was coming to an end.

We went public with this information, but predictably the mainstream news media did not give our claims credence. Among others, however, there was one savvy business leader who did respect our predictions. As president of the U.S. Chamber of Commerce, Dick Lesher had his own fingers on the pulse of middle America. Few people in or out of politics enjoy a better vantage point for gauging the public mood. The U.S. Chamber sits atop a vast pyramid of 215,000 member companies in every line of commerce in every nook and cranny of the country. In addition, more than 3,000 state and local chambers affiliated with the U.S. Chamber keep it informed about what is happening on Main Street, U.S.A. The rank-and-file members of local chambers—barbers and shopkeepers, grocers and real estate brokers, car dealers and homebuilders—are the economic backbone of this nation. Their ranks are being swelled by tens of thousands of visionary high-tech entrepreneurs in the vanguard of the digital technology revolution that is transforming our economic superstructure with quickening speed. It is a dynamic, sophisticated coalition.

Lesher's sources were telling him the same thing our field workers were telling us—that there was a mighty surge of anti-government feeling at large across the national landscape that portended great changes afoot. It was evident across all levels of society but especially conspicuous among small business-people. They had simply had enough and were determined not to take it anymore from a big government that so often seems at odds with common sense, indifferent to ordinary people, and remote from the democratic process that is supposed to assure accountability.

Sooner or later everyone feels the heavy hand of big government. The big business executive feels it when federal regulations require expenditure of hundreds of millions of dollars for burdensome paperwork requirements. Homeowners feel it when they are denied use of their property out of deference to some endangered form of obscure plant life. Working people feel it when they see their taxes squandered on foolishness, their kids denied quality education, and their neighborhoods threatened by thugs.

And small businesspeople feel it every hour of every day from contacts with a host of federal agencies that seem to have no other purpose than to impose expensive new obligations and responsibilities upon any entrepreneur who dares to pursue a vision, create an enterprise and—if really reckless—create jobs.

For many years the small business community has been accumulating grievances against big government and demanding redress from elected officials in Washington. A coalition of probusiness members of Congress has sought to respond to this legitimate plea, but for a long time we were lonely voices in the legislative wilderness. The result was a steady expansion of government into every phase of American life and commensurate growth of voter disenchantment. We all knew a backlash was building, but no one could be sure how strong it would be or when it would come.

The elections of 1994 witnessed the first full expression of a small business community that is rapidly being empowered by modern technology to communicate, coordinate, and dictate its will to the political process. Only now are political experts beginning to realize the impact of small businesses on the election, the political power they represent, and its implications for the future.

When the small business community becomes fully aroused and committed to action, as it did for the first time in 1994,

watch out! Small business has the money, the votes and—
perhaps most important—the influence in local towns, and
communities to sway public opinion in a dramatic way. In Bob
Dylan's memorable phrase, they have the power to shake the
windows and rattle the walls of Congress.

Not surprisingly, an unprecedented number of small business people sought and won seats in the 104th Congress,
where they are today the most vocal and resolute faction of
the new majority that did more in its first 100 days than any
other Congress in history. Of the 73 freshman Republicans
elected to the House in 1994, 60 were small businesspeople—
and I am not even counting the professional attorneys, accountants, and medical people who were engaged in entrepreneurial activities of one kind or another, or the former state
legislators who rose to Congress by championing the cause of
small business.

In sum, the 104th Congress is dominated by advocates of
small business who are committed to curtailing the rampant
abuses of big government. Their goal is not to destroy government but to save it. They are sensible people with a balanced
vision of the proper role of government in civilized society and
a practical attitude about what is possible. Their small business
backgrounds endow them with unique appreciation of basic
business virtues like efficiency and productivity. They are now
embarked upon a long overdue reassessment of every federal
government program. Some will be eliminated, some will be
turned over to states and local governments, and some will be
rendered more user-friendly. Nothing on the federal plate—
absolutely nothing—is above scrutiny. The final evaluations
will come, not from learned academics or inspired theoreti-
cians, but from practical small businesspeople with a commonsense attitude about what works and what does not.

This will take a long time. Many of the problems and pathologies besetting American society have complex roots in socio-

logical and economic trends that will not yield to instant analysis or simple solutions. But the first rule of government, like the first rule of medicine, should be to do no harm. Lavish government programs that do no earthly good, or which foster more pain and suffering than they alleviate, must and will be jettisoned.

The power of a focused movement inspired by common interest to influence our government has a long and impressive pedigree. It was just such movements that destroyed slavery, that endowed women with political power, and that rallied our nation to invest hundreds of billions of dollars in environmental clean-up. The small business revolution is within that honorable tradition—a focused movement of concerned citizens who recognize the threat of big government to our social, cultural, and economic integrity.

In this book Dick Lesher fully recognizes the small business movement for what it is and credited its contributions to the conservative revolution that swept into Washington in 1994. This is must reading for everyone who cares about the American political scene and the future of our great country. The small-business revolution is likely to be around for a long time, and its influence is only beginning to be felt.

PREFACE

On a business trip a few months after the 104th Congress began its work, I fell into a conversation with a businesswoman who expressed grave anxiety about what was going on in Washington. She clearly regarded House Speaker Newt Gingrich with disdain as if he were something other than an inspired political leader pursuing a popular legislative agenda, and it was obvious she felt no professional kinship with the small business entrepreneurs who eagerly flock to his banner. In particular, she was distressed by the prospect that our government might renege on its commitment to care for the poor and subsidize the arts.

Her heartfelt anxiety summoned fleeting images of the final days of ancient Rome when Alaric's barbarians were poised at the city gates preparing to violate the inner sanctum of the great empire that had remained inviolate for eight hundred years and to catapult Western society into that prolonged period of social, economic, and political regression known as the Dark Ages. She did not actually describe congressional Republicans as barbarians, but it was clear she perceived them in that light.

To my growing amazement, she asserted a vague but powerful allegiance to the big government agenda that is today held in disrepute by the great majority of Americans from all walks of life, and especially among businesspeople who bear the brunt of government excesses. Advocates of big government are rare in business. Indeed, there are few today outside the ruling cliques of Cuba, North Korea, and Vietnam who still believe government can solve society's problems. This faith, as Dr. Johnson famously said of a second marriage, is "the triumph of hope over experience."

Yet there she was—a business executive flailing away at the conservative tide sweeping Washington and its unapologetic commitment to economic growth as if it were an alien life form trying to kidnap Sigourney Weaver. I responded with a few pointed anecdotes of government ineptitude and asked her how she could maintain faith in big government amid the social and economic carnage it has left strewn across the national landscape.

"I suppose I just care about people," she replied.

I was momentarily incredulous, but the more I thought about it, the more sense it made. Indeed, her reference to "caring about people" pretty much sums up the psychology that keeps big government alive despite its conspicuous failures. To many people, the actual results of Uncle Sam's adventures in social engineering and economic manipulation are less important than their noble intent. Meaning well has become an end in itself, outweighing troubling realities that suggest big government "solutions" are causing more problems than they solve.

To some extent, that woman's attitude also reflects a schism within the business community between the managements of large corporations that accept government regulation as the price of doing business and the small business executives who cannot afford to pay that price.

But the powerful antipathy of small business toward big government and its advocates represents more than a simple objection to bureaucratic excess or even a defense of its economic interests. On a more fundamental level, it is a visceral reaction of Main Street working people against a cultural elite who impose their values upon society heedless of the consequences and who steadfastly refuse to acknowledge the often grotesque and contradictory results of their handiwork.

Within that context, partisans of big government have established generous welfare programs as an expression of their concern for poor people and turned a blind eye to the dependency and illegitimacy they foster. They have enacted ambitious campaigns to help the handicapped and disadvantaged but look the other way when their schemes are used to subsidize drug addiction and alcoholism. They embrace a variety of expensive regulatory initiatives without regard to the burden they impose on society—bankrupting businesses, destroying jobs, and undermining our economic base. They demand absolute safety in food, air, water, consumer products, and transportation, though absolute safety is not possible. They enact a devil's brew of labor laws to raise the wages of working people but do not see the marginal laborers who get priced out of the workforce. They demand equality of all people in brazen defiance of the great disparity among humanity. They celebrate all manner of "alternative" lifestyles that mock the traditional family, and then marvel at the breakdown of family life and social cohesion.

The results of this great flight from reality are strewn all about us—crime, drug abuse, family disintegration, failing schools, shuttered businesses, and a growing hard core of unemployed and unemployable vagabonds of no fixed address who tax the ability of police and social service agencies to cope with their antisocial behavior. The elite social activists who live in tony neighborhoods may not see the devastating results of their big government programs, but the struggling small businesspeople on Main Street have to live with them every day.

Small business became engaged in politics in 1994 like never before and was, in my considered opinion, the decisive force in giving the Republicans full control of Congress for the first time in forty years. Indeed, the great majority of freshman members of Congress are themselves small businesspeople with a decidedly small business view of the world.

Those who claim the 104th Congress is abandoning our nation's long-standing commitment to seek redress of social problems and economic inequity are missing the point. The small businesspeople setting the agenda for our government today are good-hearted people who care deeply about social problems. But unlike the businesswoman I spoke with on that trip, they are less concerned about motives than results.

Real concern about people demands candid analysis of reality and honest recognition of society's limitations. If we lack the wisdom and resources to resolve all of society's problems, eliminate all dangers and diseases, and alleviate all inequities, we must have the moral courage to admit honestly that reality and accept our limitations as part of the human experience.

In 1994, the American people—led by an aggressive and outraged small business community—sent a powerful message to Washington that they have grown weary of unrealistic programs that cause more problems than they solve. We are poised for a long overdue reckoning with reality.

MELTDOWN ON MAIN STREET

A POLITICAL
EARTHQUAKE

No army can withstand the power of an idea
whose time has come. —VICTOR HUGO

O n the day before Christmas in 1993, Frank Cremeans
rose early, as was his custom, to manage his small concrete business in the little town of Gallipolis, which borders
the Ohio River in the southeast corner of Ohio. "When I say
it was a small business, I mean small," Cremeans says. "I
wrote the checks, I paid the bills, I swept the floors, and when
necessary I drove the trucks." It was cold and the streets were
filled with holiday revelers, but a small business like Frank's
cannot afford to let up for a moment, not even for Christmas.

Frank was not to get any work done on that memorable day.
"I was visited by not one, not two, not three, but four separate
government agencies, each on an independent mission to
check me over and look for excuses to issue fines. There was

an inspector from the Occupational Safety and Health Administration, and another guy from the Environmental Protection
Agency, and someone from the Health Department, and then
another mine inspector, all in one day. Not one of them announced they were coming. They just showed up at my door
without any prior notice and started raking me over the coals.
They scoured my business from top to bottom looking for anything they could find to justify a citation, and you know, they
just don't feel like they've earned their pay if they don't come
up with something, no matter how nitpicky it might be. I felt
like I had been mugged, like this bunch of characters had way-
laid me on the street and took turns beating me up."

That day was to prove a turning point in Cremeans's life,
and one that portends big changes in the way our government
operates. "That day I got nothing done," Cremeans notes. "I
sold no concrete, I paid no bills, and I made no money. The
government quite simply took that entire day away from me,
and for no sensible purpose. I always ran a safe business. I
always obeyed the law. But they treated me like a criminal. I
couldn't believe it. It was just too much."

The son of a coal miner, Cremeans had worked his way
through college, obtaining a B.A. from Rio Grande University
in 1967 and a master's degree from nearby Ohio University
in 1969. Long active in local Republican politics, he had run
unsuccessfully for a seat in the Ohio legislature in 1992. Now
he raised his sights.

"The story about what happened to me was so unbelievable
that it was reported in the *Wall Street Journal*," Cremeans says.
"The publicity was embarrassing for the government agencies
and earned me a lot of sympathy. But I got to thinking about
all the other small businesspeople out there who get the same
treatment day after day and their stories don't get reported
like mine did. You keep waiting and hoping that someday
Congress will recognize what's going on and do something,

but it never happens. I figured maybe it was just up to people like me to take matters into their own hands. I decided right then and there to run for Congress."

Of course, running for Congress isn't a simple undertaking. "Now, I have to tell you that in our family, decisions aren't quite that simple. I had decided that I wanted to run, but I had to get past some key voters first—in this case my wife, my two daughters, and my son. So I went home and we all gathered around the kitchen table and I told them what I wanted to do. We talked about it for a while and then put it to a vote. My wife voted no. My son John voted no. But a father can always count on his daughters. Leigh Anne and Cari voted yes.

"That left me with the tie-breaking vote. And let me tell you, that was my closest election."

Cremeans's road to Congress was anything but easy. First he had to beat out three other contenders for the Republican nomination in Ohio's Sixth District, including a well-known state senator who the experts predicted would win in a walk. Then he had to take on an incumbent, Representative Ted Strickland, who was armed with the customary incumbent's advantages, including strong support from the party organization and political action committees. But on election day, Cremeans won election with 51 percent of the vote.

Not suprisingly, Cremeans is focusing his attention these days on small business issues, particularly with regard to reducing the regulatory and tax burdens small businesspeople must contend with. "The government has become a major stumbling block to anyone who tries to start a small business and make it grow," he observes. "We have got to change that, and we're going to."

Like Cremeans, Sue Kelly of Katonah, New York, is a native Ohioan. She was born in Lima, Ohio, and earned her B.A. from Ohio's prestigious Dennison University, which she later supplemented with an M.A. from Sarah Lawrence College.

But it was her experience as a florist that provided the basis for her education in government and informed her perspective as a small businessperson acutely aware of what is wrong with our government.

"Now, you might not think that running a floral shop would entail a great deal of involvement with government regulators," Kelly remarks. "But until you try to launch a business and create jobs, you just have no idea what is involved. At every level there are inspectors and enforcement officers looking over your shoulder, citing chapter and verse in an endless maze of rules and regulations you have never heard of, demanding all sorts of reports and forms that you are supposed to have on file all the time. You would think government would want to encourage entrepreneurs to create new enterprises. After all, that's where the new jobs come from. That's where the taxes come from. But there is no sense of that in government, none at all. It's like they see small business as the enemy."

At another time in her life—in between raising four children, doing biomedical research at Harvard University, teaching math and science at a junior high school, and working as a rape counselor and patient advocate at St. Luke's Hospital in New York City—Kelly worked in property management in Westchester County. "It was the same thing all over again. You wonder how in the world property management could have trouble with government regulators. But it's like anything else: if it's a business entrprise, if you create jobs and produce profit, government agents will be looking over your shoulder, second guessing everything you do. The Internal Revenue Service takes the attitude that it has first claim on your business's bank account. That is not what our government is supposed to be about."

Like Cremeans, Kelly finally became fed up and decided to take matters into her own hands by becoming part of the solu-

tion. But Kelly's road to Congress was even more arduous than
Cremeans's because she lives in New York's Nineteenth District, where the famous Fish family had held the congressional
seat in an unbroken chain since 1843. The incumbent Hamilton Fish, a conservative Republican, was retiring in 1994. His
son, Hamilton Fish, Jr., sought to continue the family tradition
by succeeding his father, but Hamilton Fish, Jr. was a liberal
Democrat. Despite that, the elder Fish endorsed his son's
candidacy, a touching tribute to family loyalty.

However, rank-and-file Republicans were more loyal to
party and principles than to the Fish family and were determined to keep the Nineteenth District in the party fold. Kelly
had never sought public office before, but over a period of
three decades she had worked for Republican candidates at
the local, state, and national level. In the primary, she out-
polled six men, including former Representative Joseph J. Dio-
Guardi, who did not accept his defeat gracefully. DioGuardi
challenged Kelly and Fish in the general election as a third-
party candidate. Kelly won hands down, amassing 52 percent
of the vote against 37 percent for Fish and 10 percent for
DioGuardi.

Kelly's victory is especially significant in that she defeated
competitors on both her political left and right by championing
small business issues. "The people of the Nineteenth District
cast their ballots for me because they believed in our shared
vision of a smaller, smarter government and a renewed sense
of personal responsibility. But even larger than those two principles were my credentials as a small businesswoman. Our nation's job incubators and innovators have, and always will,
come from our small business sector. As a member of the
House Small Business Committee, I am committed to improving the environment for small business nationwide."

In the 104th Congress, Kelly has encountered many like-
minded individuals from similar small business backgrounds

who share her perspective on what is wrong with our government and what needs to be changed. "This Congress reflects the vision of America's businesses—commonsense regulations, growth-based investment incentives, and a role of government as partner, not obstacle," she concludes. "From my experiences as a florist in Somers, New York, to my property management background in Westchester County, I believe I know what we need to kick-start American business and get our economy growing again."

Some might not consider Representative Dick Chrysler, the newly elected Republican from Michigan's Eighth District, to be a small businessperson because the company that made him famous, Cars and Concepts, Inc., employed twelve hundred workers by the time Chrysler sold it.

But Chrysler started that company, which alters standard automobiles into unique creations, in a corner of his living room. "People see a big, successful company like Cars and Concepts and they think it just happened by accident," says Chrysler. "But it begins with a dream and from there on it's all uphill, at least in the early going. You have to raise money, a lot of money, and investors are skeptical. They wanted to know if my idea was so great, how come the big auto companies aren't doing it. In the beginning you have no staff, no attorneys, no support of any kind. It's just you, you and your dream."

But raising investment capital was a piece of cake compared with dealing with government bureaucrats. "I couldn't believe it. It was like the government was genuinely offended that someone like me would dare to create a new business. It was just one thing after another, rules and paperwork like you wouldn't believe. It's a free country all right—as long as you have a permit. For a while there, I thought I would have to choose between building the cars and working for the bureaucrats. There just weren't enough hours in the day to do both.

Somehow we survived and prospered, but I remember thinking at the time that this was just absurd. I know the government has some legitimate functions that must be done, but many of the regulations we had to obey didn't seem to have any purpose other than to make us jump through hoops all day long. I figured there just had to be a better way to do this."

In 1992, Chrysler ran for Congress and lost to incumbent Democrat Bob Carr. But in 1994 Carr resigned his House seat to make an unsuccessful bid for the Senate, and Chrysler ran again. This time he did a better job of making it exactly clear what he was running for and what he was running against.

Chrysler offered his success at creating jobs as evidence of his fitness for office and signed on early to the House Republicans' Contract with America. Lest anyone miss the connection, his Democratic opponent, Bob Mitchell, reminded voters at every turn that Chrysler supported the Contract. The voters took note and gave Chrysler 52 percent of the vote in a contest in which two minor party candidates amassed about 3 percent of the vote between them.

As a campaigner and as a congressman, Chrysler consistently expounds his main theme that government regulations put American business at an unfair disadvantage against foreign competition. "I have spent a lifetime navigating the obstacles the federal government has created for America's businessmen and -women," he notes. "My desire to preserve for my children and grandchildren the same opportunities I have been blessed with led me to run for Congress because they deserve those opportunities when it's their turn."

Now Chrysler, who sits on the Government Reform and Oversight Committee and the Small Business Committee, is in a position to do something about the way the government relates to private business. Regulatory reform is a top priority.

"After years of putting up with dumb federal rules and regulations, I am doing something about them as a member of the historic 104th Congress. This is an entrepreneur's dream—being in the right place at the right time. We're going to turn this thing around."

Cremeans, Kelly, and Chrysler are representative of the most dynamic and fascinating freshman class to descend upon Congress since 1964, when the architects of the Great Society first came to town. The difference, of course, is that in 1964 Congress was dominated by liberals crusading to expand the power of government. In contrast, the class of 1994 is led by small business entrepreneurs who are determined to reduce Uncle Sam's influence in American life. Their arrival denotes both a watershed in the evolution of American politics and a coming-of-age for small business.

"What sets this aggressively activist class of freshmen Republicans apart is their roots on Main Street," wrote David E. Sanger in the *New York Times* several months after the 104th Congress began to make its mark. "Nearly sixty of them grew up in business, mostly small business, and think that most 'business-government partnerships' excluded them."

Of course, there have always been businesspeople in the nation's legislature, but they were usually executives of larger companies who were not especially ideological or eager to challenge the establishment. Traditionally, most members of Congress have come from other levels of government, such as state legislatures or county councils, which are widely regarded as stepping-stones to national office. A disproportionate percentage were trained as attorneys and hence share the peculiar affinity for rules, paperwork, and procedures that characterizes the legal profession. Very few emerged from the small business community.

Though many advocates of big government—such as environmentalists, consumer advocates, and poverty workers—perceive themselves as friends of small business and profess great affection for the entrepreneurs on Main Street, those sentiments are rarely reciprocated. Small businesspeople as a group have little patience with advocates of big government.

Ironically, the large corporations that are routinely condemned by activist groups for alleged insensitivity to social issues are generally managed by professional graduates of business schools who have long since made their peace with big government. They employ legions of lawyers, safety engineers, personnel specialists, and environmental scientists to sort through the rules and paperwork imposed by Uncle Sam. I have known more than a few of them who are generally sympathetic to big government programs.

That lofty attitude is most assuredly not characteristic of the class of 1994, about half of whom hail from small business backgrounds and most of whom have never held elective office before or worked for the government in any capacity.

To cite a few other examples, Saxby Chambliss, a Republican from Georgia's Eighth District, owns a hotel; Mike Doyle, a Democrat from Pennsylvania's Eighteenth District, owns an insurance company; Mark Souder, a Republican from Indiana's Fourth District, owns a general store; Republican Senator Craig Thomas of Wyoming ran a small business; John Baldacci, a Democrat from Maine's Second District, managed his family's restaurant; Linda Smith, a Republican from Washington's Third District, was a tax consultant; Ken Bentsen, a Democrat from Texas's Twenty-fifth District, was an investment banker; Tom Coburn, a Republican from Oklahoma's Second District, was a small manufacturer of optical supplies; Republican Senator Rod Grams of Minnesota was a home builder; Brian Bilbray, a Republican from California's Forty-ninth District, owned a small tax preparation firm; Tom Latham, a Republican from Iowa's Fifth District, was an executive with a seed company; Mark Foley, a Republican from Florida's Sixteenth District, founded a restaurant; J. C. Watts, a Republican from Oklahoma's Fourth District, owned a property management firm; George Radanovich, a Republican from California's Nineteenth District, was a vintner; Republican Senator James Inhofe of Oklahoma was a real estate developer; Mark Sanford, a Republican from South Carolina's First District, is part owner of two real estate businesses; Wes Cooley, a Republican from Oregon's Second District, formed his own pharmaceutical distribution company; Edward Whitfield, a Republican from Kentucky's First District, owns an oil distributorship; Jack Metcalf, a Republican from Washington's Second District, owns a bed-and-breakfast; and Mark W. Neumann, a Republican from Wisconsin's First District, was a home builder.

Many others were involved in small business issues one way or another. Michael P. Forbes, a Republican from New York's First District, once worked with us at the U.S. Chamber of Commerce and more recently was a regional administrator for the Small Business Administration; Jim Bunn, a Republican from Oregon's Fifth District, was a farmer; Helen Chenoweth, a Republican from Idaho's First District, was a public affairs consultant; David McIntosh, a Republican from Indiana's Second District, once headed Vice President Dan Quayle's Council on Competitiveness, where he worked to reduce federal regulation; and Sonny Bono, the Republican from California's Forty-fourth District, known for his early career as a popular singer and more recently as mayor of Palm Springs, owns a restaurant.

These freshmen are being entrusted with unprecedented opportunities to exercise real power and share the limelight with their elders. In the House, three freshmen—Representatives Tom Davis, Republican from Virginia, Dave McIntosh, Republican from Indiana, and Linda Smith, Republican from Washington—actually chair subcommittees, something that was virtually unheard of during the forty-year Democratic reign. These assignments were not isolated but

rather part of an overall pattern deliberately designed to empower this particular freshman class. Several freshmen were
assigned to the powerful Ways and Means and Appropriations
Committees.

Interestingly, these small businessmen and -women of the
104th Congress hail from a variety of ideological perspectives.
Some are traditional conservatives and others are former liberals who became disenchanted with the system. Some are allied
with conservative religious groups and others label themselves
social liberals and economic conservatives. They are all over
the lot on volatile social issues such as abortion.

But they are unanimous in their outspoken criticism of big
government, with which they have had much firsthand experience, most of it unpleasant.

"I ran for Congress because I felt the federal government's
heavy hand interfered too much with my life," says Representative Charlie Norwood from Georgia's Tenth District. "Like
many other small businessmen and -women, if you get the
federal government out of my business, out of my pocket, and
in general, out of my life, I'll do just fine, thank you very
much."

"During the 1980s, I remember my father telling me that
middle-aged small businesspeople should be added to the endangered species list," observes freshman Representative Zach
Wamp from Tennessee's Third District. "Throughout my adult
life I have witnessed the federal government's seeming war on
the entrepreneurial spirit and risk takers in this country. The
so-called Tax Reform Act of 1986, excessive litigation, and the
explosion of nonsensical regulations are all part of this distress-
ing campaign against the free enterprise system. Collectively
these issues boiled in me when I decided to run for Congress."

"As a small business owner, I have experienced firsthand
the oppressive effects of big government," notes Republican
Representative Mark Souder, who ran a general store in Indi-

ana's Fourth District. "This Congress is committed to ending the excessive regulation and overtaxation that limit the ability of business owners to invest in the economy and create jobs."

"Six decades of left-of-center thinking have created a condition of popular dependence on Uncle Sam as the great provider," observes Representative George Radanovich, a vintner from California's Nineteenth District. "The corrosive consequences are seen in a country where personal responsibility is a debased value, reward is not connected to effort, people aren't accountable for their actions, and failure is society's fault, not the individual's."

"We were not sent here to be typical politicians but to change things," says Representative David McIntosh, Republican from Indiana, chairman of the subcommittee on regulatory affairs. "We are much more in the tradition of citizen legislators."

These eager entrepreneurs bear some resemblance to the freshmen of the Ninety-seventh Congress that supported President Ronald Reagan's programs in the early eighties, but are as a group much more ideological. According to columnist David Broder, the Ninety-seventh Congress "wrote tax cuts and defense increases that had large, long-term consequences. But it did not uproot or reverse most government programs to nearly the extent that this Congress is doing."

THE GINGRICH FACTOR

Every election cycle produces a new crop of eager legislators determined to make names for themselves, but Congress has always absorbed them with minimal disruption of the status quo. Since time immemorial new members were expected to be seen and not heard. "To get along, go along," decreed the powerful Speaker of the House Sam Rayburn of the forties and fifties, who, like other Speakers before and since, presided over a rigid command structure based almost exclusively on seniority. Newcomers were quickly put straight about how things worked on Capitol Hill. Upstarts who didn't get the message and tried to operate outside the system soon found themselves relegated to obscure committees, denied access to pork for the folks back home, and shut out of the unofficial meetings where real decisions are made.

For forty years, the Democratic majority held sway with this rigid system. Wave upon wave of freshmen came and went—all of them ambitious politicans eager for fame and power—without disrupting the established order of Congress. Like tree limbs falling into a bog, they made a few ripples and quickly sank from view. Many years later a few hardy survivors emerged as chairmen of powerful committees. Only then, assuming they still remembered why they had run for Congress in the first place, could they aspire to actually change things.

This will not be the fate of the 1994 freshman class if Speaker of the House Newt Gingrich has anything to say about it. Gingrich has never been a "get along, go along" kind of guy. In fact, he has persistently bucked the establishment from the day he first arrived in Congress. As an obscure member of the minority in a time when it seemed like the Democrats had a ninety-nine-year lease on the House, Gingrich earned notoriety by standing in the well of the chamber late at night, long after most of his colleagues had gone home, hurling verbal stink bombs at the majority leadership for the entertainment of C-Span viewers. Many thought he was crazy, and he is—crazy like a fox. Before long everyone in Washington knew who Newt Gingrich was and, more important, what he stands for. In a world of fence-sitters and deal cutters, a person with conviction stands out.

House Speaker Tip O'Neill of Massachusetts was not amused by Gingrich's shenanigans, and on one memorable occasion ordered the House camera crew to pan the empty chamber during a Gingrich monologue—a clear violation of House rules—so that C-Span viewers would know other members of the House were not actually there listening to the brash young Georgian.

But Gingrich was not discouraged. He continued his denunciations and had the last laugh a few years later when he exposed abuse of office by O'Neill's successor, Speaker Jim Wright of Texas, who subsequently was forced to resign. For a sitting Speaker of the House to be forced from office was an extraordinary event, rendered all the more amazing because an obscure member of the minority made it happen.

House Speakers O'Neill, Wright, and Wright's successor, Tom Foley, were the last of a breed that, for better or worse, belongs to history. The takeover of the House by the Republicans, combined with the rise of Gingrich to the Speaker's chair, put an end to the forty-year Democratic reign, and with it the old way of doing things. For better or worse, the people's House will never be the same.

Gingrich rose to power through forceful intellect and extraordinary energy in defiance of the seniority system, and he is no more enamored of it now that he is in charge. By any impartial standard of reckoning, he is unique. For the first time in ages, we have a Speaker of the House who can actually speak. He is motivated as much by intellect as politics and can hold his own in debate with anyone. He writes books, champions lofty principles, and takes stands on difficult issues. He meets personally with kids from D.C.'s troubled inner-city schools to listen to their problems and reassure them about their future. He faces squarely the nation's tough long-range challenges, such as runaway entitlement programs, that send lesser political lights scurrying for cover. He has convictions and the courage to back them up. If Gingrich were an advocate of big government, his image would be chiseled on Mount Rushmore by now.

Anyone who doubts Gingrich's formidable powers need only contemplate how quickly and deftly he assumed the Speaker's gavel. Despite virtual abandonment of the rigid seniority system to enforce discipline, Gingrich enjoys greater control of the House than any Speaker since Rayburn. He inspires loyalty not by intimidation but by inclusion. He doesn't drive people, he leads them. He makes it clear to all that he is looking for competence, commitment, and loyalty and that any member of the House is welcome to play on his team, regardless of how long they have been around or intend to stay. The freshmen responded favorably to this message, as did their veteran colleagues.

The shift in the prevailing ideology of Congress, at least in its attitudes toward business, could not be more profound. The Republicans taking over as chairmen of the House and Senate committees that deal with issues of concern to business had an average probusiness rating of 90.1 percent in 1993, compared with 21.3 percent for the Democrats they replaced. (These data are based upon key business issues selected and tracked by the U.S. Chamber of Commerce.) In the House, the incoming chairmen had an average rating of 87 percent compared with 16.5 percent for the outgoing Democratic leadership. In the Senate, the comparable ratio was 93.5 percent to 26.4 percent.

New Senate Majority Leader Bob Dole had a probusiness rating of 100 percent in 1993, compared with 27 percent for outgoing Senate Majority Leader George Mitchell and only 20 percent for new Minority Leader Thomas Daschle.

On the key Senate Labor and Human Resources Committee, new Chairwoman Nancy Kassebaum of Kansas had a 91 percent probusiness rating in 1993, compared with former Chairman Edward Kennedy's 36 percent.

On the House side, Speaker Newt Gingrich had a 91 percent probusiness rating in 1993, and new House Majority

Leader Richard Armey had a 100 percent rating, compared with only 9 percent for House Minority Leader Richard Gephardt.

Overall, the new Senate committee chairmen voted for business 93.5 percent of the time in 1993, compared with only 26.4 percent for the senators they replaced. In the House, new committee chairmen voted for business 87 percent of the time compared to only 16.5 percent for the chairmen they replaced. Overall for both houses of Congress, the shift was from 21.3 percent probusiness in 1993 to 90.1 percent probusiness in 1994. The shift could not be more striking.

The result is something new on the Washington scene: an exuberant majority following a dynamic leadership in pursuit of a clear vision for change. That vision reflects the small business view of the world that most of the freshman class of 1994—eleven senators and eighty-seven members of the House—brought to Washington, enhanced by a work ethic that will not yield easily once it is committed. In practice it means "drive and determination," says Representative Wamp of Tennessee. "Getting up and staying with something. We are the conscience of the 104th Congress."

A REMARKABLE SYMMETRY

Gingrich demonstrated his vision and courage well before the 1994 elections when he and other members of the Republican leadership issued the Contract with America, a bold plan of action for the new Republican majority of the House, which at the time was little more than a gleam in Gingrich's eye. More than a few critics thought the Contract was foolhardy because it gave the Democrats a specific target to campaign against. But Gingrich has a keen sense of the political currents moving through the political heartland and carefully calibrated the Contract to catch the wave. The results speak for themselves. The Contract galvanized a momentous political upheaval and set the stage for a historic first hundred days for the 104th Congress.

At about the same time Gingrich and company were drawing up the Contract with America, I and other officers of the U.S. Chamber of Commerce were working with our members around the country to hammer out our National Business Agenda for 1995–96. This is a standard operating procedure that enables our grassroots membership to define the small business positions on important issues. We conducted a "national town meeting" via satellite from our headquarters in Washington to hundreds of downlinks at state and local chambers of commerce to discuss key issues with our rank and file. We followed up this meeting with a survey of those who attended that videoconference, and a second survey of all members via *The Business Advocate*, the U.S. Chamber's supplement to *Nation's Business* magazine. The result was a comprehensive statement of business priorities and opinions on key legislative and policy issues—what business thinks our government should do.

There was no coordination or communication between the U.S. Chamber of Commerce and the House Republican leadership. Indeed, by the time we learned about the Contract with America, the National Business Agenda was a done deal. But the two documents are virtual clones, and critics can be forgiven for suspecting collusion. The phrasing was different and the priorities varied, but identical core elements lay at the heart of both the Contract with America and the National Business Agenda. Each called for a smaller federal government, more accountability from public officials, fewer federal regulations, less paperwork, lower taxes, and greater reliance on the private sector.

Though this similarity was not especially surprising, it did seem to align us squarely with the Republican Party at a time when the Democrats still controlled both houses of Congress and none of us expected them to relinquish that control anytime soon. Like most citizens, we had gradually come to regard the Democratic majority of the House as a permanent fixture of the Washington scene. The Republicans achieved a slim majority in the Senate for six years in the early 1980s, during the Reagan years, but otherwise the Democrats had held sway in both chambers since 1954 and did not appear in any imminent danger of losing their grip.

For the record, the U.S. Chamber of Commerce—like all major business organizations—has always been studiously nonpartisan. Our members, who cover the waterfront politically, demand this political neutrality.

Also, given the long dominance of Congress by the Democrats, any overt Republican partisanship would be extremely foolish. Business needs friends in Congress regardless of who is in the majority at any given time. In fact, up until this year business political action committees gave the lion's share of their political contributions to Democrats, many of whom were and remain strong advocates of business interests.

It is established policy for the U.S. Chamber to endorse candidates for Congress based on their votes on key business issues and the support they receive from chambers of commerce in their states and districts. We abstain from a few races where neither candidate seems preferable to the other in terms of business issues, but we never make a call based on party affiliation, and we absolutely never get involved in presidential elections.

But the similarity of our National Business Agenda to the Contract with America put our predominantly small business members shoulder to shoulder with Republican candidates for Congress at a critical moment when the great controversy over health care reform already had them up in arms against the Clinton administration.

The Health Care Hubbub

Without question, the Clinton administration's health care reform plan was the single most polarizing issue that forced small business to the barricades in almost frantic opposition to it, and hence by default into the Republican camp.

Health care was and remains a priority issue for business because most Americans obtain health insurance through their employers. This system evolved during World War II when business was not allowed to offer higher pay to attract employees in a tight labor market and hit upon the idea of offering benefits such as health insurance as an employment inducement. But what began as an enlightened innovation has become an albatross around the neck of the free enterprise system. A typical business spends an amount equal to half of its annual earnings on employee health insurance. Older manufacturing companies are burdened with tremendous health care costs for retired employees. Many smaller companies simply cannot afford to buy health insurance for employees and remain in business.

Meanwhile, the costs of health care continue to race ahead of inflation with no end in sight. Thus, when President Bill Clinton came to office promising a comprehensive approach to health care reform, the business community, including the U.S. Chamber of Commerce, was receptive and interested. Influential people I know and trust assured me Clinton was a "new Democrat" who was probusiness. The Democratic Leadership Council, which was created to bring the Democratic Party back into the political mainstream, claimed Clinton as one of its own. We met with President Clinton and his top advisors, and initially we were favorably impressed.

Furthermore, there were some vital national issues upon which we agreed and worked effectively with the administration. Foremost among these was the North American Free

Trade Agreement (NAFTA), which President Clinton, after some initial hesitation, strongly supported. Once he committed to NAFTA, he fought diligently to get it through Congress despite the outspoken protests of his constituents in organized labor.

In the great national debates about international commerce, politics truly did make strange bedfellows. There are many conservatives in this country who frequently align themselves with business on important issues but do not understand that we are part of a world economy. It is a grotesque and potentially disastrous gap in their educations. Every barrier to international commerce is a pothole in the road to prosperity. We must never forget the infamous Smoot-Hawley Tariff, which virtually closed our shores to imports and brought on the Great Depression in an era when foreign trade was not nearly as vital to our economy as it is now. We need no repeats of that dreadful experience.

President Clinton came down on the right side of free trade and stuck to his guns, but there is a curious schizophrenia to the Clinton administration. Even as it worked with the Republicans against its own organized labor constituency to promote NAFTA and, later, the General Agreement on Tariffs and Trade, it pushed through Congress the largest tax increase in history and launched a domestic agenda that resembled something from the Great Society of the 1960s.

For a period of several months the administration managed to conceal its internal contradictions, but health care stripped away its cover, brought it out into the open, and set off the chain reaction that destroyed the forty-year Democratic reign of Congress. The flash point of this reaction was the small business community.

Initially everyone—including small business—was eager to work with the administration on health care reform. I personally met several times with Ira Magaziner, the head of the administration's Health Care Reform Task Force, and invited him to the U.S. Chamber to take questions from a business audience. Like the president himself, Magaziner is articulate and persuasive. He was well received, and we hoped the administration would offer constructive proposals for reforming health care.

There is much agreement among businesspeople about the problems with our health care system that must be dealt with. Costs are out of control and millions of people have no health insurance. Workers cannot easily tote health insurance from one employer to another, and people with preexisting conditions cannot get it for any price. Unscrupulous lawyers routinely plunder the system for their own financial benefit, and the threat of lawsuits by itself is a major factor driving up health care costs. Significant changes are definitely needed.

At the same time—and this is a mighty important qualification—we have the best health care system in the world and do not want to lose it or compromise it. Rumors that the Clinton administration would propose a massive federal takeover of health care provoked great anxiety, especially among small businesspeople. The world is full of governments that have attempted to regulate health care, and the result is always rationing of mediocre service. For all of its faults and attendant inequities, the free enterprise system is far and away the most efficient and effective system we know of for managing anything, be it production of Hula Hoops or delivery of health care. A federal takeover of health care was never an option to business.

But to our consternation, a big government takeover is exactly what emerged from the secretive deliberations of the Clinton administration's Health Care Reform Task Force, a 1,342-page Rube Goldberg concoction that looked like an electronic schematic for a Trident nuclear submarine. The very idea that the American people would accept such an improbable plan for anything as important as health care was simply unthinkable.

We were aghast and our members were outraged. Long before we broke off negotiations with the White House, our members were telling us in no uncertain terms they wanted no part of that plan. Our policy committees, which had been working diligently to develop sensible positions on the various aspects of health care reform, were caught behind the curve of small business opinion and were soon scrambling to catch up. "Small businesspeople had been upset about federal mandates for many years, but that health care plan galvanized them as never before," notes Jim Barrett, president of the Michigan Chamber of Commerce. "That was the most overwhelmingly negative response to a government initiative that I have ever seen. It was scary."

"We had better grassroots support against Hillarycare than on any other topic I can remember," says John Fowler, president of the Colorado Springs Chamber of Commerce. "It had a huge impact. It was one of those issues that really gets people excited."

"It was small businesses that led the charge against health care changes—which would put them at a disadvantage against their bigger brethren," David E. Sanger wrote in the *New York Times*.

At the U.S. Chamber, we went to great pains to make certain the individuals tying up our telephone lines and fax machines with outraged condemnations of the Clinton health care plan were truly reflective of our overall membership, which only a few months before had expressed strong interest in reforms. We surveyed all 215,000 of our members directly. More than 40,000 filled out and returned the questionnaires, an unprecedented response to a survey of that type. There was no doubt where they stood. They wanted no part of the Clinton plan.

Even in liberal parts of the country the fallout was conspicuous. Austin, Texas, for example, is a university town often referred to as "the Berkeley of Texas," notes Glenn West,
president of the Austin Chamber of Commerce. "But even
here we saw the conservative tide making itself felt, especially
among small businesspeople. We came out against the Clinton
health care plan."

"The interesting thing about that reaction was its reso-
nance," says Barrett of the Michigan Chamber. "It wasn't just
a one-shot deal about health care. For a lot of small businesspeople, the health care thing was the straw that broke the cam-
el's back. They called and faxed legislators in Lansing and
Washington. They held press conferences and wrote letters to
the editor. We got impassioned letters from pizza parlors and
small manufacturers. They asked, 'What can we do?' Not just
on health care but on other things, too. They got engaged,
many of them for the first time, and they have stayed engaged."

"We definitely have momentum," says Austin's West. "Now
it is up to small business to keep it going."

"As a state legislator and longtime small businessman, I can
say without qualification that small business was more active
politically in 1994 than in any of my previous campaigns," remarks Representative Doc Hastings, who won election in 1994
to Washington's Fourth District seat. "That activity was evident by more businessmen getting involved individually rather
than through their business associations, although that activity
also had increased. There is no question this was a major factor
in my victory."

A RISING FORCE

The sudden eruption of small business in the wake of the
health care debacle, and the decisive impact it had, were in

part an outgrowth of a recent trend in American business that has received little attention from the news media but which bears great significance for the future of our economy and our political system: the small business sector of the economy is growing like a house afire.

Small companies have always provided a cornucopia of essential products and services to the economy, and created about half the jobs, but were never before able to fully translate their numbers and resources into commensurate political power. They lack the resources and administrative support that larger companies routinely employ to influence the political process. Most small businesspeople have more than enough work to do and problems to worry about without taking on the federal government. A typical response of small businesspeople to the latest new outrage from Washington was to shrug, grumble, and return to work.

Similarly, while politicians and commentators as a matter of course have given lip service to the importance of small business to the economy over the years, the vital ingredient of political power was missing and the small business agenda tended to get bogged down. Big business, with its professional lobbyists, orchestrated agenda, and well-endowed political action committees was the dominant voice in the business community.

But the business world is changing dramatically, and the voice of small business is resounding with a new clarity, immediacy, and aura of power. All of a sudden millions of entrepreneurs are speaking with one voice. It took an external threat—the Clinton administration's health care reform plan—to evoke that new voice and demonstrate its clout, but now it is clear to one and all that there are new kids on the block who command respect and attention.

To some extent this phenomenon reflects the rapid growth of the small business community. The sheer numbers of small businesses, always impressive, are today truly awesome. A full 21 million business tax returns were filed in 1992. Most are sole proprietorships, but about 5 million are distinct business entities employing more than 60 million people.

Of the 215,000 member companies of the U.S. Chamber of Commerce, 96 percent have fewer than one hundred employees, 83.6 percent have fewer than twenty-five, and 72 percent have fewer than ten. The small business component of the local chambers of commerce affiliated with us is even more conspicuous. Overall, small businesses make up 99.7 percent of all employers, account for 52 percent of sales, provide 50 percent of private sector output, and account for 54 percent of all employment, according to the Small Business Administration. They own 41 percent of all business assets, carry 41 percent of all business debt, and control 42 percent of all business net worth.

But those numbers don't convey the real story. Small business is on a roll. It is without question the most dynamic sector of the economy, creating the bulk of new jobs. Every day brings fresh reports of large- and medium-size corporations slashing payrolls in a continuing trend of downsizing. Between 1989 and 1991, large companies with five hundred or more employees contributed a net gain of only 122,000 jobs. During that same period, small companies employing four or fewer employees created 2.6 million net new jobs.

In manufacturing, those small businesses with four or fewer employees were the only ones to create new net jobs. In all other business size categories, job creation either remained constant or actually declined.

Not surprisingly, small business is becoming more active in exporting to other countries. In 1992, only about 12 percent of small businesses were exporting. That percentage has already crested 25 percent, according to the Small Business Administration, and is expected to exceed 30 percent by the end of the century.

It is scary to imagine the economic turmoil that would prevail in this country today, along with the social and political repercussions, if small businesses weren't creating millions of jobs to replace jobs being lost in larger companies. The vigor of the small business sector is especially conspicuous in the service sector, which added 1.9 million new jobs between 1989 and 1991, of which 1.1 million were in firms with four or fewer employees.

More recent data suggest that trend is accelerating. New business incorporations have skyrocketed from 650,000 in 1990 to more than 750,000 in 1994, a new record! Even more impressive, these start-up ventures are prospering as never before. Business failures have dropped precipitously from slightly fewer than 100,000 in 1992 to about 70,000 in 1994.

Much of this trend is attributable to a strong economy, but there are other forces at work. The rapid growth of small business reflects the application of advanced technology to the modern workplace in myriad ways that greatly enhance efficiency and productivity and at the same time foster countless new opportunities that eager entrepreneurs are rushing to take advantage of. The leaders of the small business revolution are increasingly found in high-tech industries, which on average have twenty or fewer employees.

More than a few of these are executives who have been cut loose from larger corporations during downsizing and who reacted by launching their own ventures. A typical example is Toby Malachi of Indianapolis, Indiana, who was once an executive with General Motors but saw his job eliminated in a round of downsizing. Malachi then launched his own enterprise, Malachi Diversified, Ltd., a trade development company that identifies business opportunities and alternative markets around the world. "Electronic digital communications are spawning entire new categories of small business," says Malachi. "Downsizing leads more and more people to create their own firms, while the new technologies are creating more opportunities for new small firms."

This focus on sophisticated technology is reflected also in the wage levels of the new small businesses. According to research supported by the Small Business Administration in conjunction with the 1995 White House Conference on Small Business, "the most recently hired workers in small firms are obtaining a major share of high-wage jobs" even as "large firms continue to shed high-wage jobs." Thus, the new activism of small business is partly a function of the growing ranks of small firms and also of the growing sophistication of small business people. They are on the cutting edge of the new communications technologies and know how to use them in ways that scarcely could be imagined even a few years ago. One such innovation—and one that carries momentous implications for our political system—is to begin tying small businesses all over the country together in a seamless web of digital communications technology.

Just as creative use of modern technology is enabling small businesses to compete more effectively with larger companies, it also enables them to communicate easily and inexpensively with each other on a regular basis and to bring their combined influence and resources to bear on important issues that affect the business environment. It used to take weeks or months for an organization like the U.S. Chamber of Commerce to inform its small business members about a proposed law or regulation that would prove especially costly or impose new requirements on them; now we can do it within a few hours and begin getting their feedback almost immediately.

Politicians are generally pretty quick to pick up on this sort of trend and more than a few, even those with no direct experience in small business, are actively seeking to get ahead of the small business curve.

"There is no question about the political activism of small business, and the candidates now are aware of it," observes Ron Zooleck, president of the South Shore Chamber of Commerce in Quincy, Massachusetts. "They are being courted by politicians as never before. The politicians want to meet with small businesspeople, not big businesspeople. Small business is finally realizing it can make a difference, a big difference."

Zooleck's chamber routinely hosts luncheons and breakfasts for political candidates, including presidential candidates, to address, often with five hundred to one thousand small business activists in attendance. "We try to explain to the politicians that profit is not a four-letter word but that loss is," says Zooleck. "All those taxes and regulations force small business to keep nonproductive employees on the payroll. We have no trouble getting huge turnouts for political events because small businesspeople care deeply. My twenty-four hundred members, ninety-five percent of whom are small, are fully engaged in the political process."

According to Jack Camper, president of the Metropolitan Tucson Chamber of Commerce, "Small business is fed up with big government looking over its shoulder at everything it does and confiscating its hard-earned dollars for wasteful government programs. Our members are overwhelmed and frustrated by big government. We are extremely active politically. We look for and support probusiness candidates and keep track of what they do.

"By the fall of 1994, dozens of small businesspeople from across our region were actively trying to elect me to represent them when the 104th Congress convened to clean up the legacy of the Great Society and other federal government excesses," says Representative Wamp of Tennessee. "In the new

Congress we are rolling up our sleeves to get small business-people off the endangered species list."

"I believe the 1994 election was about two things," notes Representative Souder of Indiana, "curbing the ever-expanding role of the federal government in people's lives and getting a handle on our out-of-control national debt. The best way to control both problems is to reduce federal spending."

Perhaps the most important ingredient of small business's newfound political muscle is its extraordinary credibility with the American people, which politicians and parties can only envy. Overall there is a profound sense of estrangement and disappointment afoot in our country. According to a 1995 survey by Democratic pollster Stan Greenberg and Republican pollster Fred Steeper, more than 70 percent of the American people do not trust our government to do the right thing. That pattern is consistent among liberals and conservatives, men and women, the affluent and the poor.

But according to a survey conducted about the same time by Louis Harris & Associates, the public has great confidence in small business proprietors. A full 42 percent expressed "a great deal of confidence" in small business proprietors and another 47 percent "some confidence" in them. In contrast, only 24 percent expressed "a great deal of confidence" in religious institutions, 19 percent in big business, and 15 percent in the news media.

Clearly, there is more to this movement than a group of businesspeople looking out for their own economic interests. The American people identify with small business in a personal way. They see in entrepreneurs the qualities and values that made this country great and that hold the greatest promise for the future. They see resolute individuals taking on tremendous odds in pursuit of dreams. To the extent that small business aspires to impose its basic values on the government in Washington and apply common sense to federal programs, it is doing the people's will and Congress knows it.

The emergence of small business as a decisive force in national politics has come at a propitious moment when a variety of conservative groups have mobilized against overreaching government. But small business is the dominant force in this coalition because it is endowed with a specific agenda for change that enjoys overwhelming public support. According to Representative Frank A. LoBiondo, a freshman from New Jersey's Second District, "This Congress has finally recognized that no government-run welfare program, health care program, or crime bill can do as much to solve our social problems as a private sector job."

It seems a foregone conclusion that the 104th Congress, given its powerful small business core, will address a series of vital issues that small business has been clamoring about for years. Among these will be a tougher Regulatory Flexibility Act requiring federal agencies to consider the special needs of small business when issuing new regulations; a modified product liability law limiting the legal exposure of firms with twenty-five or fewer employees; a revamped Small Business Administration loan program; a broadening of the number of home-based businesses that can claim home-office tax deductions; lower estate taxes; and a clearer independent contractor rule.

But the first priority of the 104th Congress is to clean up the mess left by a generation of runaway government. At issue are a host of federal programs that have long since lost sight of their original purpose and are long overdue for a reckoning with reality.

2

IN QUEST OF COMMON SENSE

*When Ralph Nader tells me that he wants my
car to be cheap, ugly, and slow, he's imposing a
way of life on me that I'm going to resist to the
bitter end.* —TIMOTHY LEARY

A bank in Kansas City was ordered by federal regulators to install a braille keypad on an automated teller machine at a cost of $5,000 to comply with the Americans with Disabilities Act (ADA). "Keep in mind this is a *drive-through* we're talking about," the bank's lawyer told the *Wichita Business Journal*.

A plumbing company in Boise, Idaho, was penalized by the Occupational Safety and Health Administration (OSHA) because its employees ignored safety rules while rescuing a fellow worker from a collapsed trench. Because they did not wear their hard hats or shore up the trench before pulling the man to safety, OSHA inspectors proposed a $7,875 fine. (Following a tidal wave of adverse publicity, OSHA vacated the penalty.)

After John Schuler, a Montana rancher, shot a grizzly bear that charged him on his own property, he was fined $4,000 for violating the Endangered Species Act. In Alaska, where bears frequently threaten people, the Environmental Protection Agency (EPA) banned sale of BearGuard, a popular pepper spray residents frequently use to ward off pesky bears, because the EPA had never actually tested it for effectiveness against bears. "The EPA admits that the spray is probably safe to eat if not to smell," said Senator Frank Murkowski, Republican from Alaska. "It seems like you can use it on a dead bear, you can use it on a bear stew, but you cannot use it on a live bear if the bear is after you."

Even more un-bearable is the tale of the Food and Drug Administration's action against John McCurdy's small herring smokehouse. After twenty years and 54 million flawless fillets, McCurdy had to shut down his business and lay off twenty-two employees because the FDA demanded he install $75,000 worth of new equipment. He didn't have enough money.

Blair Taylor invested $150,000 in his new fifteen-employee Barolo Grill in Denver, Colorado. Four days after he opened, federal regulators demanded a redesign to better accommodate the disabled. Taylor wonders why they made him install an expensive ramp to eight tables in the rear of his grill when the front sixteen tables were already accessible to the disabled. Do the feds truly imagine some night Taylor will be deluged with enough wheelchair patrons to fill twenty-four tables? Before his ordeal was finished, Taylor spent $48,000 in additional construction costs, $19,000 in legal fees, and $16,000 in fines and penalties.

Or consider the Daniel Lamp Company of Chicago, whose troubles with the Equal Employment Opportunity Commission (EEOC) got national airing on the CBS program *60 Minutes*. The EEOC made Daniel Lamp pay $123,000 in back pay to workers who had applied for jobs but were not hired. The company, which is in a Hispanic neighborhood, employed 21 Hispanics and 5 blacks, but that wasn't good enough for EEOC bureaucrats, who said the company should employ 8.45 blacks.

Perhaps the most infuriating tale of sheer regulatory zaniness is recorded in Philip K. Howard's book *The Death of Common Sense*. In the winter of 1988, Mother Teresa's Missionaries of Charity sought to renovate an abandoned building in the South Bronx to use as a shelter for the homeless. The nuns appropriated $500,000 to repair the abandoned building, but after eighteen months of pleading their case before one city agency after another, they were told they would have to have an elevator installed in the building at an added cost of $100,000. The nuns do not, as a matter of religious conviction, use such modern conveniences, but city bureaucrats were implacable. No elevator, no shelter. Mother Teresa's nuns abandoned plans for a shelter.

Finally, the Consumer Product Safety Commission (CPSC) has gone to great pains to distance itself from reports that it once proposed a regulation to require holes in five-gallon plastic buckets to reduce chances of children drowning in them. The story sounded like a classic case of run-amok regulators going off the deep end, but the CPSC assured Congress and the public that the story was a fabrication.

Not according to Representative David McIntosh, Republican from Indiana, who has the evidence in hand against the CPSC. "On July 8, 1994, the CPSC issued an Advanced Notice of Proposed Rulemaking regarding the manufacture of five-gallon plastic buckets," he said. "The CPSC's notice proposed six ways to prevent the risk of drowning, including the construction of buckets that 'cannot retain liquid,' i.e. leaky buckets. The CPSC abandoned this regulatory lark only after substantial public criticism."

Outrages such as these have entered modern folklore as

Americans of all walks of life lament regulatory foolishness that at times seems to border on insanity. According to a survey by Times-Mirror, since 1987 the percentage of citizens who believe the government controls too much of our lives has jumped from 57 percent to 69 percent. Within the business community, exasperation with government regulation is virtually unanimous.

What's missing from anecdotes of bureaucratic lunacy is a sense of judgment or common sense to ameliorate the application of arbitrary rules. The culture of bureaucracy does not encourage judgment, initiative, or common sense. To the contrary, bureaucrats are held accountable for enforcing the letter of the rules that have long since become much too voluminous, dense, and impenetrable for any normal person to grasp and understand.

Their dilemma is an ancient one, described by Saint Paul in a famous letter to the early church at Corinth: "Not of the letter, but of the spirit; for the letter killeth but the spirit giveth life." Saint Paul recognized that no matter how carefully rules and laws are written, there will always be times when they either don't apply to the specific circumstances at hand or they produce results inimical to what was intended. On those occasions, enforcement of the rules simply must be tempered with judgment.

But bureaucrats have scant leeway to exercise judgment. Government managers have precious little direct authority over their subordinates, either to reward performance or punish failure. Thus, they are naturally reluctant to endow subordinates with even more independence of action. The results, as these anecdotes confirm, often are absurd.

In fairness to the regulators, many anecdotes of regulatory excess are exaggerated, and the complexity of rules is made necessary by the legal environment the regulators are obliged to work in. Also, it is to be expected that some crazy things will happen when so many people are enforcing hundreds of confusing laws and thousands of often illogical and contradictory regulations. That said, the regulatory outrages against common sense continue unabated, and the pressing need for reform remains unsatisfied.

One benchmark of the level of regulatory activity in Washington is that the total number of bureaucrats employed by the fifty primary federal regulatory agencies swelled from 28,000 in 1970 to 127,842 in 1993. Meanwhile, the annual cost to taxpayers for keeping them in paper and red tape rose from $4 billion in 1970 to $13.5 billion in 1992 (as measured in constant 1987 dollars).

Another measure of expanding regulation is the sheer number of rules now amassed in the *Federal Register*—which in 1970 ran to 114 volumes and 54,834 pages. By 1993, it consisted of 202 volumes and 131,803 pages, taking up nineteen linear feet of shelf space.

Equally troubling is the mounting burden of paperwork and reporting required by federal agencies, reliably estimated to total 6 billion hours per year. Each hour represents many dollars to the businesses that must pay someone to fill out the paper. Small businesses that do not have administrative staff to handle the paperwork complain the loudest, especially when they must deal with different agencies demanding the same information in different formats.

The growing burden of paperwork is persuasive evidence of bureaucratic indifference to the economic consequences of red tape. Virtually every federal agency issues a steady stream of recordkeeping and reporting requirements, most of them related to regulations. Indeed, it is difficult to separate the impact of paperwork requirements from that of regulations.

Congress recognized the severity of the problem in 1980 when it enacted the Paperwork Reduction Act, primarily through the efforts of Senator Lawton Chiles, Democrat from

Florida, who is now governor of the Sunshine State. The law created an Office of Information and Regulatory Affairs (OIRA) within the Office of Management and Budget to rein in Uncle Sam's paper mania.

OIRA had some success under Presidents Reagan and Bush in forcing federal agencies that require information from the private sector to first determine if some other agency already had it. Many redundant paperwork requirements were eliminated as a result of that simple exercise, but only after business groups put the heat on and kept it on.

It is the peculiar nature of the bureaucracy that sensible initiatives like this arouse great resentment and efforts at evasion. To obtain the desired information from other agencies instead of directly from businesses somehow affronts the dignity of bureaucrats who want to gather the data themselves on their very own forms and really do not care if they are forcing businesses to invest huge amounts of time and effort reporting the same data over and over to different agencies.

This concept is hard for small businesspeople to understand, but within the context of bureaucratic culture the gathering of information is deemed a worthy act in and of itself, regardless of whether the information gathered serves any viable purpose. Bureaucrats simply do not understand why others do not share their passion for paperwork.

To further cloud the issue, the Supreme Court ruled in *Dole* v. *Steelworkers* in 1990 that OIRA could control only that paperwork reported directly to the federal government. Reports to third parties, including any arm of state or local government, were off limits to OIRA review. The decision eliminated about one-third of OIRA's paperwork jurisdiction, a portion that quickly began increasing as federal agencies learned of the loophole and rewrote their rules to require reports to third parties acting in their behalf.

Business pleaded with Congress for years to rewrite the Paperwork Reduction Act to close the loophole and give OIRA expanded powers to impede unnecessary paperwork demands, but the advocates of big government in Congress refused to let it happen.

Not until the American people ordained a major shift of political fortunes did the Paperwork Reduction Act receive new life as part of the Contract with America. It sailed through Congress with the enthusiastic support of its new small business contingent and was signed into law by President Clinton. Though it did not receive much publicity, it was a major achievement and long overdue.

THE SCROOGE McDUCK THEORY OF ECONOMICS

What matters most about federal regulation is not the occasional atrocity or the number of bureaucrats or the number of pages in the *Federal Register*. The real question is what impact all of this has on our society and whether the benefits of regulation and paperwork are commensurate with the costs. There is a growing body of persuasive evidence that the regulatory bureaucracy is exacting an ever higher cost from society in exchange for steadily diminishing returns.

Economist Roger Hopkins of the Rochester Institute of Technology calculated the annual cost of regulations to American society in 1992 at $500 billion, or $5,000 per household, while economists Nancy Bord and William Laffer pegged the total of direct and indirect regulatory spending to range from $810 billion to $1.1 trillion. The latter figure is almost equal to total 1992 tax revenues collected by Uncle Sam.

Whether it's $500 billion or $1 trillion does not appear relevant to the federal regulatory bureaucrats and their constituencies, which are primarily environmental groups, labor unions, and consumer activists. They regard the questions about costs to be part of an anticonsumer, antienvironment, and anti-worker conspiracy. The very suggestion that regulations should be subjected to cost-benefit analysis is ridiculed as if such base calculations had no legitimate place in public debate.

The only issue that really matters, according to regulatory advocates, is protection of consumers, workers, and the environment, and every complaint about cost, no matter how compelling, is casually dismissed as carping from "special interests."

Cost-benefit analysis is a basic management tool for private enterprise but it remains a political hot potato in Washington. Basically, it is nothing more than a simple effort to estimate what a new regulation will cost and weigh that cost against what it is expected to achieve—whether in terms of environmental protection or reduced hazards to humans. Admittedly, cost-benefit analysis is not a magic bullet to eliminate bad rules because it is often difficult to accurately estimate either their costs or benefits, but even so the advocates of big government will have nothing to do with it because it is predicated on the assumption that costs matter.

For years, I tried to fathom the mentality that simply waves off concern about the cost of regulations as irrelevant. Finally, I hit upon what I call the Scrooge McDuck Theory of Economics.

This theory is based upon a presumption that environmental and consumer activists learned what little they know about economics from some delightfully amusing Disney comic books about a fictional character named Scrooge McDuck.

Uncle Scrooge, an uncle of Donald Duck, is a tightfisted billionaire business duck who relieves stress by swimming around in a vast money bin at his corporate headquarters. He pushes piles of money back and forth with a small bulldozer and leaps happily into the mounds of cash from a diving board, swimming to and fro in a state of fiscal ecstasy.

In some manner unclear to me, this comic book vision of the corporate money bin made a permanent impression on the subconscious minds of regulatory advocates and today informs their carefree attitude toward the cost of regulations. Thus, to say that a new regulatory program will cost $20 million or $20 billion simply makes no impression on them. According to Scrooge McDuck theorists, such problems are negligible irritants. All business has to do is back a truck up to the money bin and shovel out the appropriate amount. What could be simpler than that?

It follows logically that any business, large or small, that complains is, like Uncle Scrooge, motivated by greed and indifferent to the well-being of people and the sanctity of the environment. Critics who decry regulatory costs are dismissed as deluded apologists for corporate rapacity. What difference does it make if the money bins are a foot or two shallower next month?

The basic flaw in the Scrooge McDuck theory, and hence in the attitude of regulatory zealots, is that there are no money bins. This reality impresses me as self-evident, but amazingly there are a great many citizens whose perceptions of corporations have been shaped by Hollywood images that reflect the Scrooge McDuck perspective. Indeed, when businesspeople are portrayed in movies like *Wall Street* and television productions like *Dallas*, it is almost always as sleazy characters conspiring against truth, justice, and the American way.

This is a relatively recent phenomenon on the American scene and in my view a most unfortunate one. In my youth, the captains of American industry were generally regarded with awe, if not reverence. We were taught to believe, correctly in my opinion, that men like Thomas Edison, Alexander Graham Bell, Walt Disney, David Sarnoff, and Alfred P. Sloan were enlightened agents of social and economic progress. They brought revolutionary new products to market that enhanced the quality of human life, and their innovations in management and production created wealth on an unprecedented scale. In our own times I see on the national scene a new breed of visionary entrepreneurs building on that tradition as they set the stage for a dynamic new economy to serve a new century. That they acquire fortunes in the process and work hard to keep them strikes me as unremarkable. For the most part, they are honorable people who obey the law and behave reasonably well. At the very least, their comportment compares favorably to that of moviemakers, social activists, politicians, and journalists who routinely depict businesspeople as rapacious scalawags.

In any event, all of the money that comes into corporate possession goes to pay taxes, pay employees, maintain plant and equipment, and invest in new ideas and processes. Most profitable businesses also allot funds to charity and other public service endeavors. But all of the money is spoken for.

After all taxes are paid and all expenses are met and appropriate investments in the future allotted, what's left over—if anything—is distributed among investors and shareholders. It warrants mention that the tax collector stands first in line to receive corporate largesse and is conspicuously indifferent to the corporation's bottom line. Even the most beleaguered business on the threshold of liquidation must pay taxes. It warrants comment too that the popular image of fat-cat shareholders so commonly encouraged by comic books and movies is also mostly fantasy. To be sure, there are some wealthy individual stockholders, but the biggest investors in corporate stock are pension funds or mutual funds representing the savings of working Americans.

When businesses are required to spend billions of dollars to comply with regulations, the money must be taken away from these basic categories that define the purpose and function of corporations. It cannot be taken from the part allotted to taxes. Nor is it trimmed from the expenses associated with energy, supplies, and other basic materials of commerce over which the corporation has no control. Every penny spent on regulatory compliance is taken from employee salaries, investment in new products and equipment, donations to charity and public service, or dividends paid to shareholders. Simply stated, the cost of complying with regulations is paid directly from the pockets of citizens. Every last penny of it.

MEASURING RISK

Because regulatory costs are paid in real money taken from the pockets of real people, it follows that regulators and their advocates bear a solemn responsibility to justify the spending they require. Consumers still have a right to know what their regulatory dollars are being spent for.

The simple answer, of course, is safety and quality of life. The industrial machinery and infrastructure that modern society is built upon is the source of our tangible wealth and modern conveniences, but it also produces waste that is often unsightly and potentially hazardous. It must be cleaned up and sanitized lest our environment become intolerable and our wealth a curse instead of a blessing.

It is not reasonable to expect businesses caught up in vigorous competition to expend huge amounts of money on environmental cleanup and workplace safety if the competition isn't subject to the same requirements. Thus, regulators play an important role as impartial umpires to assure that all competitors in the marketplace play by the same rules.

Likewise, the myriad consumer products we savor and benefit from, if poorly made and haphazardly serviced, can present hazards. We citizens of a modern, sophisticated society presume a right to safe and healthful jobs, environment, food, clothing, medical treatment, transportation, and consumer products. If something is sold to the public, we assume it is safe and hold the government responsible for ensuring that it is—be it a car or an airplane ride, a sandwich or a miracle drug, a stereo or a shirt.

Thus, we must begin with the presumption of a reasonable need for uniform and consistent regulation, impartially administered, and a complementary presumption that much of the cost associated with regulation is both wise and warranted. What Justice Oliver Wendell Holmes, Jr., said of taxes is equally true of regulatory costs—they are "the price we pay for civilized society."

But Justice Holmes never suggested taxpayers had no right to critique how their tax dollars are spent or to question whether they are spent wisely. Indeed, that is the most basic and frequently debated of political issues. We have now reached the point, at least according to some credible experts, that we are spending as much on regulations as we pay in taxes. It follows that ordinary citizens have a commensurate right to demand an accounting of regulatory costs as they do of taxes.

Herein lies the great dilemma of the regulators, and the real reason regulatory advocates become so agitated by the prospect of regulatory scrutiny, such as would be required by cost-benefit analyses. In a great many cases, the risk targeted by expensive regulations is so small as to be virtually invisible, and hence the benefit equally so.

Unfortunately, the public is not always able to make sensible judgments about relative risk, as when people fear flying more than auto travel. This vacuum of rationality endows regulators and their constituencies with great power, and they frequently succumb to the temptation to abuse it.

For example, the Department of Transportation (DOT) ordered General Motors to recall an estimated 6.3 million trucks sold between 1973 and 1987 that are still on the road to relocate their fuel tanks, reducing their susceptibility to fire and explosion in case of impact. This massive recall, which could cost upward of $1 billion, may possibly save thirty-two lives during the remaining time the vehicles are on the road, according to the DOT's analysis. That works to about $31 million per life in a highly hypothetical calculation that may or may not bear any direct relationship to reality. Simple logic demands that before a $1 billion expenditure is required, specific benefits be guaranteed. But the cost means nothing to the DOT bureaucrats or the consumer activists backing the recall. It is strictly a "money bin" calculation.

Here in Washington, D.C., the local Metro system was ordered by the federal Department of Transportation to invest $30 million installing bumpy platform edges at all seventy-four of its rail stations to provide a more effective warning to blind commuters. When the system was built in 1976, Metro installed eighteen-inch-wide granite edges, which have proven quite effective in alerting blind passengers they are near the edge. Metro's general manager Lawrence G. Reuter resisted the order to tear them out and replace them with different edges, telling a House subcommittee that Metro was "the safest rail system in the country." James Gashel, speaking for the National Federation of the Blind, said Metro's existing guards were more than adequate, but the feds were implacable.

The $30 million cost of installing new edges would have come from increased fares imposed on Metro riders, almost all of whom are working people. The upper crust does not ride public transportation. It was a classic example of abuse of regulatory power by bureaucrats with no sense of the devastating impact such requirements can have on communities.

This particular story has a happy ending, for Uncle Sam finally backed off on April 25, 1995, permitting Metro to employ a less costly system for improving the safety factor for vision-impaired patrons. The announcement was greeted as a triumph of common sense over bureaucratic intransigence by the Clinton administration, but it was—like the belatedly updated Paperwork Reduction Act—an achievement of the no-nonsense, small business–oriented contingent in the 104th Congress.

MEDIA COLLABORATION

The regulators could never get away with such foolishness without the active cooperation of the news media. In a peculiar way, the frequent red flags raised about alleged hazards in our air, water, food, and workplaces fill a pressing need of electronic journalism for subject matter. Television reporters have a lot of airtime to fill. Hysterical claims of invisible hazards in air, water, and food make convenient filler on slow days. Better yet, there is little chance the news agency will be sued for false reporting because the existence of such hazards can never really be proved or disproved.

The activist groups who demand aggressive regulation have become quite expert in fulfilling this need of the electronic media to their own purposes. By stirring the pot constantly, scaring consumers and workers half to death, they rally new members and presumably are able to increase their cash flow and political influence.

The result has been a series of increasingly bizarre and destructive blowups that generally foment a lot of confusion before petering out. Some of the more memorable ones include the partial evacuations of Love Canal, New York, and Times Beach, Missouri, both of which now appear in hindsight to have been unnecessary. Likewise, the scare associated with the nuclear accident at Three Mile Island was blown out of proportion. No one was killed or even harmed, except for the emotional trauma caused by the exaggerated reports of peril.

More recently the outrageous brouhaha about Alar on

apples in 1989 was instigated by an irresponsible environmental group and ably abetted by a famous actress, Meryl Streep. It began when traces of a pesticide named Alar, well within the EPA's stringent standards, were discovered in apple juice. Irresponsible environmentalists proclaimed an imminent health hazard, and uncritical news media accepted the claim as factual, reporting it in frightening terms. Suddenly apple consumption dropped through the floor, with predictable results for apple growers and retailers.

In the wake of the brouhaha, an ad hoc group of fourteen prominent organizations representing one hundred thousand microbiologists, toxicologists, veterinarians, and food scientists, issued a statement that the health risk from approved agrochemicals were "negligible or nonexistent" and that "the public perception of pesticide residues and their effects on safety of the food supply differs considerably from the facts."

But by the time the EPA established that Alar was safe and there was no need for panic, millions of dollars had been lost and many apple growers had gone bankrupt. Again, there was no apology forthcoming from those who orchestrated the Alar debacle. The regulatory crowd simply refuses to see the costs of their work in human terms.

"It is commonplace to observe that risk is ubiquitous and inescapable," Peter Huber wrote in *Regulation* magazine some years ago. "Every insurance company knows that life is growing safer, but the public is firmly convinced that living is becoming ever more hazardous. Congress, understandably enough, has been more interested in the opinion polls than in the actuarial tables."

To a great extent, the political upheaval of last November was a direct result of the regulatory excesses that are taking a toll on our way of life and driving ordinary Americans to distraction. *Time*'s Hugh Sidey spoke of it in a postelection *Crossfire* program in which he cited anecdotes he had heard on the campaign trail from farmers, retailers, and aviators. "Wherever you went in these last few months, you heard this litany from almost any family, anybody, of the intrusion, the burden of government," Sidey said. "There is a crisis."

"The United States has become an overregulated society," the *Washington Post* opined in a lead editorial on March 26, 1995. "It is not just the volume or even the cost of regulation that is the problem but the haphazard pattern—a lack of proportion. The government too often seems to be battling major and minor risks, widespread and narrow, real and negligible, with equal zeal. The underlying statutes are not a coherent body of law but a kind of archaeological pile, each layer a reflection of the headlines and political impulses of the day. The excessive regulations discredit the essential. Too little attention is paid to the cost of the whole and the relation of cost to benefits."

THE GREATEST REGULATORY BURDEN

But by far the greatest regulatory nightmare disturbing the dreams of small businesspeople from coast to coast is not the prospect of a surprise OSHA inspection or a new mandate from the Environmental Protection Agency or a charge of discrimination filed with the Equal Employment Opportunity Commission. Rather it is the possibility of an audit by the Internal Revenue Service.

Without question the IRS is far and away the most hated and feared of all the regulatory bureaucracies. It is impossible to converse with any small businessperson for more than ten minutes about his or her enterprise without eliciting expressions of outrage about the tax system and its chief enforcement agency. I deem it inevitable that the 104th Congress, at the behest of its aggressive small business freshmen, will eventually turn its attention to the IRS and the infamous tax code.

Of course, the very concept of a popular tax collector is as oxymoronic as jumbo shrimp. The tax collector was created by government to take our money away from us and is empowered with sufficient authority to do it. To be within the clutches of the IRS and whipsawed back and forth by its confusing and often contradictory mandates is the very definition of helplessness. No one who gets caught up in that star-chamber proceeding is likely to forget it.

While a few individuals are at times able to shield at least some of their income from the IRS's grasping palms and get away with a few "creative" deductions, such freedom is not available to small business entrepreneurs, who must account for every penny that passes through their hands in the sure and certain knowledge that every deduction they claim will be second-guessed by abusive IRS bureaucrats who seem to feel a proprietary right to all business income and take perverse delight in the anguish of small entrepreneurs unaided by tax lawyers.

To be sure, our government is obliged to extract a certain amount of tax dollars from the citizens in order to fund the basic services expected of government—maintenance of public roads, national defense, criminal investigations, and the like. As Justice Holmes said, taxes are the price we pay for civilization. It's a fact of life.

But the amount of our personal and business income that the government confiscates and the inscrutable labyrinth of increasingly complex tax regulations that the IRS enforces are fair subjects for debate and legislative remedy.

That debate promises to be an interesting one because there is an overwhelming body of evidence to suggest that our government takes more of our income than it has a legitimate right to or is good for the country. As for the complexity of our tax code, it is, quite frankly, obscene.

HISTORICAL PERSPECTIVE

From the vantage point of the late 1990s, it seems almost comical to look back at the beginning of the century, when there was no income tax. Congress had enacted one during the Civil War, when the government hovered near bankruptcy and desperate measures were clearly called for, but a few years after the war the Supreme Court ruled it unconstitutional. That was the end of the income tax, or at least should have been.

But the citizens of our great country just had to have an income tax, so in 1909 a vigorous group of tax advocates persuaded Congress to approve an amendment to the Constitution authorizing one, and by 1913 the thirty-sixth state legislature ratified the Sixteenth Amendment, which overrode the Supreme Court and set those IRS agents in motion.

That remarkable achievement seems more bizarre with every passing day. In recent decades, we have seen a variety of enthusiastic attempts to amend our Constitution. In each case, the cause at hand—guaranteeing equal rights for women, banning abortion, requiring a balanced federal budget—has been aggressively championed by well-financed movements that enjoyed broad public support. Yet not one of those amendments has been ratified by the required three-fourths of the states to become part of our basic legal code. Our ancestors were somehow able to overcome all the opposition that stood in their way.

I personally find it more than a little interesting that a few years after that they amended the Constitution again, this time to forbid the manufacture and sale of alcoholic beverages. It is as if they took a long hard look at what they had done with the income tax and decided they were drinking too much.

To be sure, the avowed purpose of the Sixteenth Amendment was one familiar to all of us in our own time—to soak the rich. The voters assumed that the income tax would apply only to the very wealthy few whose conspicuous consumption was deemed offensive by the social and moral arbiters of that era. Anyone earning more than the then princely sum of $3,000 per year had to pay 1 percent of it to Uncle Sam.

The social and moral arbiters of our own time, mostly self-appointed liberal advocates of big government, are still singing the same song, insisting every effort to cut taxes is a plot to help the rich. Last year, for example, the Republican majority of the 104th Congress proposed a stringent budget designed to eliminate the deficit within seven years, which included an exceedingly modest $250 billion tax cut stretched out over the same time. The Democrats attacked it over and over again as a "tax cut for the rich."

As columnist Robert J. Samuelson opined, the Democrats' carping about tax cuts for the rich "merely disguises their own unwillingness to confront the budget deficits." It is much easier to criticize the other fellow's tough decisions than to offer realistic alternatives.

In any event, any tax reduction is of necessity going to offer the most benefit to upper income people if only because they are the ones who pay most of the taxes in the first place. According to The Tax Foundation, in 1993 the wealthiest 5 percent of Americans paid 47.3 percent of tax revenues collected by the government, up from 37.3 percent in 1983. Overall the top 10 percent of income earners, who collectively receive 39.1 percent of the income, carry 58.8 percent of the tax load. People at the bottom of the income ladder bear a minuscule percentage of the tax burden.

TAX CODE COMPLEXITY

At various times, in what appears to be some sort of basic superstitious ritual, Congress ventures forth on yet another highly publicized campaign to allegedly "simplify" the tax code. The usual result is to add new layers of regulatory interpretations to the several hundred pages already on the books and make yet more work for the legions of auditors and accountants who crowd around the tax code like camels around an oasis.

The last time Congress engaged in this ritual it actually did reduce the number of basic tax rates that ordinary income is subject to, but it did not actually simplify the tax code in any fundamental way. Nor did it actually contribute anything useful to understanding the increasingly complex code that has long been indecipherable to most Americans.

No group is more frustrated by the tax code's enigmatic and ever changing emphasis than small business. What small business wants from Congress, and has pleaded for many times, are some rational answers to basic questions pertaining to small enterprises. One is deductibility of the use of personal property, such as rooms in one's residence or a personal vehicle, for business purposes. The rules governing such decisions seem to move with each change of wind direction or personnel turnover at IRS headquarters.

Another tax priority for small business is a practical guide to determine when an independent contractor is an employee, a bit of information millions of small businesspeople would just love to get their hands on. Every year thousands of small businesspeople are informed by the IRS after the fact that those independent contractors they have been using are in reality their employees, a revelation that inevitably comes as a surprise to both them and the contractors.

More than a few small businesses have been driven into

bankruptcy by such rulings, which small businesses, unlike larger corporations, can rarely afford to challenge. It takes too many years and too many thousands of dollars in legal fees.

The complexity of the tax codes is often a subject of jokes and merriment, but it is no joke to millions of small business-people whose enterprises all too often depend upon the caprice of individual IRS auditors who, like most federal bureaucrats, rarely exhibit sensitivity to the burdens they impose on private business. What's missing in the IRS rules is a commonsense awareness that real people cannot obey laws they do not and cannot understand. There is simply no reason for these outrages to continue any longer. An all-out campaign to truly simplify the tax code, and answer basic small business riddles, is long overdue.

THE FATAL FLAW

But more galling still than the unnecessary complexity of IRS rules and regulations is the sheer burden of taxation in this country, which is totally out of line with what is necessary and conducive to steady economic growth. Many observers in all parts of the political spectrum, including some respected voices on the right, continue to make the case that we are, as a nation, undertaxed.

The reality testifies otherwise. When all levels of taxation are taken into account—local, state, and federal—the combined tax take is about 35 to 36 percent of total Net National Product, which, as computed by The Tax Foundation, is Gross National Product minus depreciation of physical assets. As such it is comparable to the nations of Western Europe, which are even now wrestling with the legacy of decades of overly generous social programs and burdensome taxes.

Even that doesn't tell the real story, because in Western Europe the citizens generally receive a full range of benefits and services for their tax dollars. In this country private business and individuals pay out of their own pockets for supplemental education, training, health care, and security that are provided by the governments of Western Europe.

In that sense, comparing our tax load to that of Great Britain, Germany, France, or Sweden is comparing apples and oranges. After paying our governments an equivalent rate of taxation, we end up having to pay twice for basic services because our government is so wasteful and incompetent. Let there be no mistake about this salient point—the small business revolution is based upon the deeply held belief that our tax laws are too complex and our taxes are too high and the IRS is too arbitrary.

The experience of politicians who deny this reality has been universally discouraging. Walter Mondale promised to raise taxes and took a thrashing at the polls. President Reagan agreed to accept tax increases immediately in exchange for spending cuts to be named later. The tax increases sailed through without a hitch; we are still waiting for the spending cuts. President Bush challenged anyone who doubted his steadfast opposition to tax increases "to read my lips." When he broke that pledge, his political goose was cooked.

There are three compelling reasons why both parties should make tax cuts a basic element of their political agendas and remain committed to them.

First, both parties have promised to cut taxes. As former President Bush learned to his sorrow, the voters take note of these promises. Second, as we move through this period of downsizing in the public sector, eliminating many activities and jobs, we need an expanding private sector to pick up the slack, and lower taxes are key to that. Nothing can thwart the goal of a balanced budget faster than a recession that dries up tax revenues even as it requires ever higher spending for social aid programs.

Third, and most important, our tax rates are much too high. If there is one conspicuous economic fact we have firmly established over the last twenty years, it must surely be that high marginal tax rates discourage economic investment and growth. The most critical factor in economic growth is an expanding small business community testing new products and services, fostering innovation, and creating new jobs. Confiscatory taxes and overly complex tax regulations make it exceedingly difficult for small business to perform this basic function.

THE REGULATORY DILEMMA

Government is hard-pressed to respond to the regulatory crisis because it is the source. In its zeal to ameliorate the human condition, protect everyone from everything, and find the money to pay for it all, our government is steadily eroding our standard of living and driving an increasing number of citizens to exasperation. It is clear this system is out of control and that comprehensive reforms are long overdue.

But this problem took a long time to create and will take a long time to resolve. The 104th Congress, true to its small business orientation, is working on legislation that will make it more difficult for federal agencies to impose expensive new rules without due consideration of their economic impact. But any bill that gets signed by President Clinton will probably be watered down to the point that it is meaningless.

Meanwhile, tens of thousands of existing rules remain on the books to be dealt with, and much regulation is required by a variety of regulatory laws that must be reviewed and amended one by one. Few laws require cost-benefit analysis for new rules and many actively prohibit it.

It will take a lot of time and work to achieve substantive changes in the regulatory system. The challenge is complicated by a federal regulatory bureaucracy that is difficult to control under the best of circumstances and that is institutionally resistant to the kind of changes we so desperately need. Also, everyone in Washington knows the drive for reforms could easily be wiped away in the next electoral cycle. Indeed, the advocates of big government who believe we need even more regulations are conducting a delaying action while they wait for changes in the political arena.

In an eloquent essay on Frederick the Great of Prussia, the nineteenth-century British historian Thomas B. Macaulay observed that Frederick's subjects came to despise him, not because of his endless wars and frequent acts of tyranny but because of his persistent efforts to regulate their personal behavior. "He firmly believed he was doing right," Macaulay wrote. "Yet this well meant meddling probably did more harm than all the explosions of his evil passions during the whole of his long reign. We can make shift to live with a debauchee or a tyrant, but to be ruled by a busybody is more than human nature can bear."

Federal regulators mean well, as do their defenders among various activist groups, but they are driving people crazy. Their handiwork has evolved into a regulatory morass that is strangling our economy and choking off the lifeblood of our most vital small business sector. What meager benefits we derive from this regulatory system are vastly outweighed by the damage it does to our economy and social structure.

3

SAVING THE ENVIRONMENT FROM ENVIRONMENTALISTS

❖

*"Environment" and "safety" are fine objectives,
but they have become sacred cows about which
it is almost heresy to ask whether the return
justifies the cost.*   —MILTON FRIEDMAN

"What we have here," said actor Strother Martin in a famous line from *Cool Hand Luke* just after he knocked Paul Newman for a loop, "is failure to communicate."

In early 1993, the Environmental Protection Agency (EPA) and Amoco Oil Company concluded an unprecedented collaborative study of plant pollution demonstrating an incredible potential for cost savings and improved efficiency in environmental cleanup if only government and business would communicate and cooperate.

Their inability to communicate says a lot more about government than it does about business. The EPA and other government agencies that enforce environmental rules are locked into a 1970 mindset that regards business as an enemy. As a result, government officials making key decisions affecting business remain incredibly ignorant about the way business operates and oblivious to the often devastating impact ill-conceived regulations have on our economy.

The collaborative work between the EPA and Amoco began with a chance encounter of two old friends in 1989, one employed by EPA and the other by Amoco. Their conversation soon turned to shared regrets about the large amount of money being squandered on environmental programs without commensurate result. Soon Deborah Sparks of Amoco and James Lounsbury of the EPA were nudging their respective employers toward a radical new notion of cooperation instead of confrontation.

Amoco offered its refinery in Yorktown, Virginia, to serve as a test case to determine if a more efficient, sensible regulatory approach could be found. There were many-layered walls of distrust to overcome on both sides and more than a few setbacks along the way. Amoco was concerned lest the EPA should use access to the company's proprietary information as a basis for punitive legal action. The EPA feared its regulatory mission would be compromised. As one EPA official noted, many agency employees perceive themselves as the good guys going after the bad guys. Various EPA divisions appeared to be scheming to abort the collaborative project as if it were a threat to the agency's culture (which it was).

Fortunately, then EPA administrator William Reilly weighed in at a crucial moment to keep the project on track. The results were shocking, at least to people who care about squandered money. For example, it was determined that Amoco would be required by EPA regulations to spend $54 million to reduce hydrocarbon emissions from its Yorktown refinery over the ensuing four years, though the company could achieve the same emission reduction in other ways for only $10 million. The company would be required to spend $41 million to upgrade its wastewater treatment plant to control benzene emissions, but it could eliminate four times as much benzene by spending $4.7 million on its barge-loading operations.

The Yorktown project dramatically underscores what is wrong with our regulatory system. There is among government rank-and-file employees a profound distrust of business and indifference to the cost of regulations. It is rooted in history, embedded in bureaucratic culture, and encouraged by outside groups.

The Yorktown project was deemed so successful that Reilly's successor, EPA administrator Carol Browner, announced a "Common Sense Initiative" to extend this method of cooperation to projects in six other industries. She deserves credit for this initiative, but it will take more than one successful experiment to alter the EPA's antibusiness culture.

It is a critical challenge, for of all the realms of government regulation, none has greater impact on our economy and way of life than environmental regulation. Estimates of the total cost vary wildly from $200 billion to $500 billion per year. The EPA itself offers a much more modest estimate of about $115 billion. "However, estimates by [the] EPA tend to be low," wrote Philip H. Abelson in *Science* magazine, the official publication of the American Association for the Advancement of Science. "Municipalities have reported instances in which real costs exceeded EPA estimates by a factor of twenty or more."

Abelson's observation has the ring of truth if only because EPA bureaucrats, like their counterparts at other regulatory agencies, consistently demonstrate a conspicuous indifference to the cost of their rules and a smug conviction that complaints about costs are driven by corporate greed and indifference to higher values—namely protection of the environment. But whatever the actual cost of environmental regulation may be, it is large and commands attention.

A JUST CAUSE

Environmentalism surged to the fore of the nation's consciousness in 1970—on the first Earth Day—in response to an increasingly obvious problem. In the preceding quarter century, between the end of World War II and 1970, our industrial output soared and with it the wretched refuse of industrial pollution. Likewise, growing population placed increasing demands on electric generation and water treatment facilities. Many of our lakes and rivers degraded into colorful cesspools of industrial effluents and raw sewage. (In one notorious incident, the Cuyahoga River, which flows through Cleveland into Lake Erie, actually caught fire.) The air in many major cities was filthy and getting worse. At times, the concentration of particulates in the air of some cities became dense enough to conduct electricity. In sum, our nation was headed toward ecological disaster.

A growing number of Americans believed we needed a massive nationwide assault on pollution, and only the federal government could do it. When Congress was reluctant to act, President Richard Nixon created the EPA with an executive order. Congress soon reinforced the president's order with a series of increasingly aggressive environmental laws. From that time to now, we as a nation have been engaged in a vigorous and highly expensive campaign to restore our environment as closely as possible to its pristine state and to remove recognized health hazards from air, water, and land.

The story that yearns to be told is how successful we have been. Indeed, it is one of the best-kept secrets of modern times. The much-publicized Earth Summit in Rio de Janeiro in 1992 should have been a celebration of how environmental awareness had finally come into its own, punctuated with a series of flattering tributes to the United States, which has served as pathfinder in this momentous undertaking.

Over the past twenty-five years we have spent a significant percentage of our Gross Domestic Product cleaning up our air, water, and land. Thousands of miles of once befouled rivers and streams today run fresh and clean. Aquatic life again teems in lakes where once nothing could survive. We have slashed soot and dust emissions by nearly 90 percent. All new cars today must have expensive catalytic converters to reduce emissions. At great trouble and expense, we have reduced urban smog. We have invested hundreds of billions in state-of-the-art sewage treatment facilities and now enjoy one of the purest water supplies in the world. We were the first to abolish chlorofluorocarbons from consumer products, and our enlightened and progressive approach to disposal of solid waste is (or at least should be) the envy of the world. We have set aside huge tracts of forest as permanent refuges for fauna and flora and aborted many promising economic projects to protect endangered species. Rarely in the annals of human history has any people committed so much of its treasure to such a noble cause. Our commitment to the environment ranks with the Marshall Plan as persuasive evidence that ours is an enlightened society committed to higher values.

But the environmentalists gathered in Rio, including a large contingent from U.S. environmental groups, did not celebrate these achievements or praise the United States. To the contrary, the assembled activists took turns lamenting the sorry state of Mother Nature, predicting imminent catastrophe and blaming the West—mainly the U.S.—for all that is wrong.

Therein lies the great paradox of environmentalism and the root source of the controversy that today surrounds nearly all aspects of environmental regulation. The more successful the environmental movement becomes, the more radical its partisans become. As one environmental goal after another is achieved, the environmental movement raises new issues and objectives. The irony is that our very success seems to breed more extremism in the environmental community and greater detachment from reality.

The writer George Santayana defined fanaticism as "redoubling your effort when you have forgotten your aim." Much of the environmental movement today appears to fall well within that definition. Extreme action inevitably provokes reaction, and in this case there is a growing body of opinion across the political spectrum that the environmental movement has lost its moral and ethical compass.

The environmental movement is long overdue for some serious soul searching and reconciliation with reality. Unfortunately, many within the movement possess an evangelical fervor for their cause reminiscent of religious fundamentalism and just as resistant to rational discussion.

Command and Control

From the outset, the EPA employed a direct, no-nonsense "command and control" approach to environmental cleanup. The EPA launched our national environmental crusade by laying down the law to polluters across the board. The EPA dictated what had to be done, when it had to be done, what the result had to be, and how progress was to be documented to the satisfaction of the federal government. The EPA's approach was brutal, expensive, overbearing, and incredibly effective.

In a time when the sources of pollution were so clearly identifiable and their insult to the environment so undeniable, the EPA's direct approach worked well. Industry and municipalities raised a mighty howl about the cost and protested the EPA's arbitrary decrees, but there is no denying it worked. In a few short but intense years we began to atone for centuries of environmental degradation.

But because something worked effectively in the 1970s doesn't necessarily mean it is the right approach for the 1990s. The Volkswagens of 1970 did not get as many miles per gallon as the Cadillacs of today do. The best office typewriters made by IBM in 1980 are now quaint relics of a distant past. Many standard medical treatments of 1970 would in 1995 provide grounds for charges of malpractice. Likewise, the techniques and concepts that drove the EPA's enforcement in the 1970s are not appropriate for the environmental challenges of the 1990s or reflective of our more sophisticated attitudes regarding efficiency and productivity.

Unfortunately, there is a mentality in the federal bureaucracy that defies change and rejects innovation. The EPA has evolved into a vast operation with more than ten thousand employees spending billions each year just to administer its programs. The EPA administers eleven major laws and enforces well over nine thousand regulations, a total that climbs daily. Some of the laws entrusted to the EPA's enforcement, unlike most regulatory laws, contain highly specific requirements that are, in effect, regulations in their own right. Thus, even if the EPA were inclined to apply reasonable interpretation to rules, it is in many cases forbidden by law from doing so.

For example, in 1991 Congress enacted environmental legislation requiring cities to remove at least 30 percent of the organic waste from incoming sewage before treating it. This put the citizens of Anchorage, Alaska, in a bind because its sewage contains little organic matter to remove. But unless the city met the requirement, it would have to build a $135 million treatment facility. Rather than do that it invited two local fish processing plants to dump five thousand pounds of fish viscera into the sewage system. The city then removed it, satisfying the requirement.

Further compounding the problem is the changing nature of the EPA's tasks. Clearly visible insults to the environment—dirty air and water, industrial and municipal waste—have been dealt with. The problems that remain tend to be more subtle and difficult to define. The EPA's vast arsenal of bureaucrats and lawyers enforcing laws and regulations is increasingly engaged in what might be described as "witch hunts" after increasingly small and often hypothetical threats to the environment and health. It is in this controversial effort that the EPA's traditional command and control approach is stirring up so much confusion and outright animosity among the regulated—businesses, school systems, and local governments.

Interestingly, the primary targets of the EPA's regulatory power today are not large industries, which have long since installed air and water treatment equipment, but small businesses and local governments. Municipalities are required to fund compliance with 419 rules deemed "essential" by the EPA and to monitor for more than 130 chemicals in their water supplies, some of them at levels of parts per billion. Needless to say, many towns and counties lack the money and expertise to fulfill these requirements, not to mention the lawyers and administrative workers needed to service the EPA's rapacious appetite for paperwork.

Similarly, small businesses must carefully identify, monitor, and inform employees about the potential effects of hundreds of chemicals and other substances. Neighborhood filling stations, laundries, and print shops suddenly find themselves facing an avalanche of rules and reporting requirements. Failure to obey all the rules can lead to massive fines, and the rules are constantly changing.

The city of Rockville, Maryland, not far from where I live,

must spend $1.5 million of its own money to handle sludge left over from filtering drinking water. Though the sediment comes from the Potomac River, where Rockville gets its water, it can't be returned to the river but rather must be hauled to a landfill. Not only that but the city must test its water for an ever expanding list of potential contaminants, which means it must invest $300,000 in a new testing facility and a resident chemist to perform the tests.

Our waterways today are remarkably clean, thanks to years of regulation and hundreds of billions of dollars, but the pollution that remains presents special problems. Most of it comes from so-called nonpoint sources such as runoff from farms, construction activity, and urban storm water. Those things are hard to measure and even harder to control.

Even so, environmental advocates are demanding stricter rules to require an inflexible pursuit of "zero discharge" levels of suspected contaminants. That is where the EPA and its advocates depart from the real world into never-never land and send the rest of us the bill. It is one thing to force industries and municipal government to spend billions to reduce poisonous emissions and effluents when there is overwhelming evidence it presents a clear and present danger to human health. It is something else again to force industries and municipal governments to spend their scarce resources to reduce alleged hazards that may not exist.

For example, soil tests near Columbia, Mississippi, revealed traces of a compound that the EPA defines as hazardous, about two ounces per ton of soil. The simplest and least expensive way to resolve the problem was to spread a layer of clean soil over the contaminated soil at a cost of $1 million. The EPA insisted, however, on a more expensive solution—digging up 12,500 tons of soil and hauling it away—at a cost of $20 million, which will be borne by local taxpayers.

VAGUE THREATS

The experience in Mississippi underscores what has become the most frequent source of regulatory disputes and questions about alleged health hazards. Time and time again, businesses and local governments are forced at regulatory gunpoint to spend millions of dollars, sometimes hundreds of millions, to eliminate or reduce hazards that exist primarily in the fevered imaginations of regulators.

At issue is the presence of traces of substances in food, medicines, soil, water, or consumer products that have been shown to cause cancer in laboratory animals under controlled conditions. The actual relevance of such hazards to real human life forms is hazy.

The basis of most regulatory activity in this area is found in an amendment to the 1958 Food, Drug, and Cosmetic Act named after its author, James J. Delaney, a long-dead congressman from New York. In essence, it banned use in food of any man-made substance that has been shown to cause cancer in people or animals.

That prohibition sounds good on paper and it made sense when it was enacted, but it has long since been rendered obsolete by advancing science and technology. When Delaney offered his amendment, scientists could identify traces of potentially harmful substances down to a level of parts per million. Sophisticated analysis today can identify traces of pesticides and other substances down to a level of parts per quadrillion. That means, in effect, that they can find just about anything anywhere.

The most obvious flaw in the Delaney clause is its focus on man-made substances. "The impact of such substances, however, is dwarfed by the consumption of natural pesticides from plants," said Wayne T. Brough of Citizens for a Sound Economy. "Americans eat more than fifteen hundred milligrams of natural pesticides a day, which is ten thousand times greater than the amount of man-made pesticides consumed. To put this into perspective, a single cup of coffee poses a risk of contracting cancer equivalent to the cancer risk from all man-made pesticides consumed in a year."

Also, the Delaney clause forbids any consideration of the many benefits of man-made pesticides and food additives. For example, sodium nitrites are added to meat to prevent botulism, saving thousands of lives each year, but sodium nitrites cause cancer in laboratory rats. Pesticides greatly increase yields of many food crops that are essential to the diet of our citizens, but pesticides cause cancer in laboratory rats. Literal enforcement of the Delaney clause, which is always a possibility, would basically shut down most of the nation's food supply.

Clearly, the Delaney clause makes little sense in the modern age, but regulatory activists refuse to even discuss its repeal. A major battle must be fought to get rid of it.

The entire business of basing regulations on animal tests is open to question. Scientists routinely give test animals the "maximum tolerated dose" of some suspect chemical, which is the highest dose that will not kill the animals outright.

Then they wait for a period of time to see if the animal develops tumors. If two different species of animal, such as rats and mice, develop cancer over a two-year period, the substance is formally declared a cancer hazard to humans.

All of this mumbo-jumbo masks a large vacuum of uncertainty. The National Research Council, part of the independent National Academy of Sciences, noted that "It is not known how similar the toxic responses in the test animals are to those in humans," and scientists cannot confidently predict cancer risk for "most people in the environment." The obvious fact—that humans are immune to many poisons in small doses—is deliberately left out of the regulatory equation.

Professor Richard Stroup of the University of Montana calculated the chances of being killed on the ground by a crashing airplane in the United States during a seventy-year lifespan at roughly four in one million. Meanwhile, the EPA has ordered costly cleanups, sometimes costing more than $30 million, for hazardous waste sites where the potential threat to safety is as low as one in a million.

In a book published before he joined the Supreme Court, Justice Stephen G. Breyer noted that asbestos control regulations will probably cost the economy $100 billion to save ten lives a year for forty years. That is equivalent, Breyer said, to adding $48,000 in safety equipment to each car to reduce the risk of traffic death by 5 percent.

The Department of Energy, which is now wrestling with the prospect of spending upward of $1 trillion over the next thirty years cleaning up toxic waste sites, recently released a report entitled *Choices in Risk Assessment* prepared by a nonprofit research group. "Most environmental risks are so small or indistinguishable that their existence cannot be proven," it said, adding that scientific policy is "inherently biased and can be designed to achieve predetermined regulatory outcomes."

Even when the desired regulatory outcome cannot be fabricated, the regulatory agencies still find a way to get what they want. A case in point was the 1993 EPA report attributing upward of three thousand cancer deaths per year to secondary cigarette smoke. I carry no brief for smoking, but that report was a sham. It has been analyzed and repudiated by a wide spectrum of scientists from diverse groups with no connection to the tobacco industry or financial interests in smoking. According to the respected Congressional Research Service, when the data did not meet the EPA's own threshold for identifying a hazard, the agency lowered the threshold. It treated primary and secondary tobacco smoke as identical though the latter is clearly diluted by contact with the surrounding environment.

Yet despite what an article in *Science* magazine called "fancy statistical footwork," the EPA was still able to draw only a vague and unpersuasive connection between secondary smoke and illness.

In this effort, as in so many others, the regulators are ignoring science in pursuit of what are clearly political goals. As one researcher quoted in *Toxicologic Pathology* said of the EPA report, "Yes, it's rotten science, but it's in a worthy cause. It will help us get rid of smoking."

On that basis the Occupational Safety and Health Administration has sought to issue a rule banning smoking in the workplace—a rule that would effectively draft every employer in the country into an antismoking police force. The costs of building thousands of separate smoking rooms and of the endless litigation that would ensue are simply irrelevant to the regulators.

Even more bizarre cases of expensive regulatory adventures abound. For example, the Office of Management and Budget (OMB) has calculated that under the EPA's Hazardous Waste Disposal Ban, $4.2 billion would have to be spent to avert a single premature death. The OMB estimated also that the EPA's Formaldehyde Occupational Exposure Limit would require a theoretical $119 billion to prevent one premature death.

Duke University economist W. Kip Viscusi said that if the nation's entire economic output were devoted simply to preventing our 94,500 accidental deaths that occur each year, the cost would work out to $55 million per life saved—which would still be less than we would have to spend complying with the EPA's rules for benzene storage, OSHA's arsenic rules, and the FDA's ban on DES.

"It has now been twenty-five years since the National Environmental Policy Act went into effect and the battle against pollution accelerated," the *Washington Post* said in a March 7, 1995, editorial. "It has produced great achievements but also notable waste. The record shows a tendency to make a couple of kinds of particularly costly mistakes. The government often overreacts to newly discovered dangers and pours disproportionate resources into hastily conceived remedies. The example that first comes to mind is Superfund, the response to toxic dumps. More broadly, the political system has trouble deciding how far to reduce a pollutant as long as any residue at all is a threat to anybody's health."

The fascination with alleged cancer-causing agents is shared across the regulatory bureaucracy, but the EPA is the biggest regulatory agency, and no other has done more to propagate the highly dubious notion that anything that causes cancer in laboratory animals at incredibly high levels of exposure is by definition hazardous to humans.

This premise came under fire in 1983 when *Science* magazine published an article by Bruce N. Ames, a respected biochemist at the University of California at Berkeley, asserting that normal healthy diets contain high levels of known carcinogens, sometimes at levels several thousand times those of manmade carcinogens, such as those left over from pesticide applications. Ames provided evidence that the human body can routinely repair damage caused by exposure to low levels of carcinogens, which fact undermines the key premise of much federal regulation.

He noted that more than five hundred chemicals found in roasted coffee can cause cancer in laboratory rats—if given in large enough doses. "This does not mean coffee is dangerous," he said, but only that the tests are so sensitive that they identify negligible risks. "Nature's pesticides, in fact, are found in levels of parts per hundred or parts per thousand, while man-made pesticides are present at levels of parts per million or parts per billion. The man-made pesticide residues currently allowed in our diet don't represent, in my opinion, any significant cancer hazard to the public."

In 1984, *Science* published a letter signed by eighteen academicians, union officials, and environmentalists accusing Ames of "trivializing" cancer risks and said "such strategies are applauded by corporations resisting regulation of their carcinogenic products and processes."

"Obviously, you don't want every chemical company to dump their garbage out the back door," Ames responded. "But I don't like this attitude that any businessman is going to poison his grandmother for a buck. There are incentives to have integrity and to *not* make carcinogens."

More than ten years after Ames's analysis, which has never been disproved or repudiated, the EPA continues to coerce businesses, farmers, and cities into spending untold fortunes to test for the smallest trace of man-made pesticides in an exercise that, so far as anyone knows, serves no valid purpose.

THE ASBESTOS HOAX

But the granddaddy of all phony health scares, and one for which the EPA bears full culpability, is the great asbestos hoax that has cost our society tens of billions of dollars and continues to this day, despite a virtual consensus among experts— including the EPA's own resident scientists—that it is all a big mistake.

The asbestos scare was instigated by the late Dr. Irving Selikoff of the Mt. Sinai School of Medicine in New York, who years ago became convinced the nation was facing an epidemic of asbestos-related disease because World War II shipyard workers, who had been exposed to huge concentrations of asbestos, demonstrated high levels of illnesses known to stem from exposure to asbestos. (It bears mention that the workplace conditions that prevailed at that time were an aberration driven by wartime emergency.)

There were two discrepancies in Selikoff's data that should have raised warning flags. First, the shipyard workers were exposed to the deadly blue and brown varieties of asbestos, and in extraordinarily high concentrations. The most common variety of asbestos, accounting for 95 percent of that used in buildings today, is the white variety that poses little threat to humans, at least in terms of marginal exposure. Second, there was a high incidence of cigarette smoking among the shipyard workers, which in conjunction with exposure to blue and brown asbestos is known to have a highly carcinogenic effect.

Selikoff's allegations set off a spate of lawsuits against asbestos manufacturers, many of which were driven into bankruptcy. Others continue to shell out money. As recently as October 1993, ten large asbestos manufacturers paid $200 million in damages to fifteen thousand school districts.

Public schools were probably the greatest victims of the asbestos hoax because of understandable concerns raised by anxious parents. In the fall of 1993, New York City schools were closed for two weeks while the city spent $83 million on asbestos inspections and removal. Total spending nationwide on asbestos removal from schools, according to the National School Boards Association, has passed $10 billion and may reach $30 billion. (Removal of asbestos from schools is required by law, so Congress is the primary culprit in this foolishness.)

By 1985, the weight of scientific evidence was undermining the case against asbestos. New data showed the level of asbestos fibers in buildings, even where there was flaking of asbestos around steam pipes, was less than in the ambient air outdoors. Indeed, asbestos is a prime example of how marginal exposure to carcinogens does not cause disease. All of us are exposed to asbestos but only a few develop asbestosis or mesothelioma, the type of lung cancer generally associated with asbestos exposure.

But Selikoff persisted in his campaign against asbestos, aided and abetted by labor unions and environmental groups. The antiasbestos campaign was and remains convincing evidence of how fanatical and indifferent to the public good the regulatory zealots can be.

In 1990, another round of data on asbestos exposure published in the *New England Journal of Medicine* and *Science* magazine stressed yet again that the dangers of asbestos had been grossly exaggerated. That year the EPA finally issued an updated version of its own asbestos report stating that low levels of asbestos in schools and office buildings represented low levels of risk. It pointed out an obvious fact, namely that ripping asbestos out of walls put a lot more of the stuff in the air than was there before, in effect creating a worse hazard.

In sum, there never was an asbestos cancer epidemic. "The real epidemic was fear," Mike Bennett writes in *The Asbestos Racket*. It was "spread by scientific ignorance, bureaucratic bungling, political posturing, greedy lawyers, sensation-mongering reporters, and contractors chasing the almighty buck."

Still, the corrected message was not getting through to the public, possibly because the EPA was somewhat sheepish in seeking publicity for it. In 1992, the EPA published yet another report, this one acknowledging it had made matters even worse by issuing confusing and conflicting guidelines.

But by 1993, the EPA was back in the hands of the regulatory activists, who are reluctant to call further attention to the asbestos hoax and to this day continue to countenance the expensive and pointless removal of asbestos from schools and other public buildings. While our public schools go begging for money to pay teachers, buy computers, and repair leaking roofs, they must squander countless millions in homage to the regulatory zealots who, true to the Scrooge McDuck Theory of Economics, refuse to acknowledge the economic impact of their actions on ordinary people.

GLOBAL WARMING

The first Earth Day celebration in 1970 brought frequent warnings of a new "ice age" that would be brought on by continued abuse of the environment. Today we have come full circle with an even more frequently repeated warning that we are headed into an era of global warming driven by the same pollution.

If true, it could spell big trouble for many people, and not just those living in seaside cottages. The champions of global warming theory insist the threat to humanity is real and severe, and demand massive changes in the way society functions in the developed world. If that means we have to cease making cars and shut down factories, the alarmists contend, so be it. But after all the false alarms environmental activists have raised in the past quarter century, it is only reasonable to take a long hard look at the global warming theory to separate facts from hyperbole.

Global warming occurs when carbon dioxide and some other gases, such as methane and nitrogen oxides, accumulate in the atmosphere. The gases pass solar infrared radiation but reflect the earth's radiation. A common analogy is that of a greenhouse trapping heat. As the quantity of gases increases, more heat is trapped. Some trapped heat is necessary to sustain life, but excessive accumulation can lead to warming.

Greenhouse gases are produced by a large range of natural and man-made processes throughout the world. Five major gases are usually discussed, with primary emphasis on carbon dioxide because it is produced in large quantities from many sources. Methane is increasingly mentioned, but while many of these gases occur naturally, it is the man-made emissions that have come under scrutiny.

Our knowledge of earth's temperature covers only a tiny sliver of the planet's history and then only certain parts of the planet. Historical records indicate the earth has had countless eras of alternating hot and cold. Only after the last ice age did modern civilization, such as it is, evolve. Based on analyses of glacial ice core samples, the Council on Environmental Quality concluded that atmospheric carbon dioxide was far higher 125,000 years ago, without the benefit of auto emissions, than it is today.

From 1900 through 1939, the earth warmed; from 1940 to 1970 it cooled. This heat-cold cycle may be natural and the changes we see taking place nothing more than the usual ebb and flow of temperature changes.

On the other hand, it could be the start of a trend. Some computer models suggest greenhouse gases may increase world temperatures from two to seven degrees Fahrenheit over the next fifty years. This could cause a shift in rainfall distribution in middle latitudes such as the American Midwest, increase the likelihood of drought, threaten agricultural production, and dry up inland lakes and rivers. As the polar ice cap melts, a rise in sea level would flood coastal cities, disturb water salinity, and destroy wetlands. One positive reaction to an increase in carbon dioxide often mentioned is an increased growth of plant life, which absorbs more carbon monoxide.

The volcanic eruption of Mount Pinatubo in the Philippines a few years ago threw a monkey wrench into everyone's calculations of global warming. The biggest eruption of the century, it sent a plume of volcanic particles into the atmosphere that within weeks encircled the world. Scientists at the U.S. National Oceanic and Atmospheric Administration predicted the plume would cause worldwide temperatures to drop by one degree over a period of three years, and by four degrees in the tropics.

The notion that human activities are damaging the earth's atmosphere sufficiently to bring about an overall increase in sea level temperatures, thus melting the polar ice caps and flooding coastal areas, has become so entrenched in popular mythology that it defies critical analysis. Anyone who raises questions about or challenges the assumptions of global warming is dismissed as a corporate apologist or an antienvironmental crank.

An engaging young writer named Gregg Easterbrook, a contributing editor to *The Atlantic Monthly* and *Newsweek,* has written a remarkable book, *A Moment on Earth: The Coming Age of Environmental Optimism,* that brings long-needed perspective to many contentious environmental issues. Easterbrook admits a basic contention of the environmentalists: that the carbon dioxide content of the atmosphere is today 25 percent higher than it was one hundred years ago. However, Easterbrook points out that carbon dioxide has always made up a tiny percentage of the atmosphere—some 290 parts per million a century ago versus 350 parts per million today. "In absolute terms, human-caused emissions of carbon dioxide have only increased the amount of this gas in the atmosphere by 0.006 percentage point," Easterbrook wrote. "It's quite common to hear environmentalists express dismay over the 25 percent statistic; rare to find them bringing up the 0.006 side of the equation."

Global warming overall is a very good thing. Without it, the world would be sixty degrees Fahrenheit colder. "The standard estimate is that water vapor accounts for 99 percent of natural global warming," Easterbrook wrote. "The remaining 1 percent of the greenhouse effect stems from carbon dioxide and other gases, which are themselves mainly products of nature, not man. Natural processes, such as volcanic eruptions and the decay of plants, add around 200 billion tons of carbon dioxide to the air annually, while human activity, mainly power production, automobile use, and the burning of forests, adds about 7 billion tons."

Thus, carbon dioxide accounts for only 1 percent of the greenhouse effect, and man-made carbon dioxide accounts for only 4 percent of that 1 percent—with the man-made part increasing at a rate of about 1 percent a year. According to Easterbrook, "This works out to the human impact on the greenhouse effect being roughly 0.04 percent of the total annual effect. That is, 99.96 percent of global warming is caused by nature, 0.04 percent is caused by people. The present rate of increase in human-caused greenhouse impact, meanwhile, works out to about 0.004 percent per annum of the total effect."

Easterbrook was careful to disavow any assertion that man-made gases play no decisive role in global warming, for no one can make such a claim with certainty. It is clearly an area in which our fears are outrunning scientific knowledge. Reports of holes in the ozone layer above Antarctica warrant concern, as do reports of massive disruptions of the southern ice cap. It is wise and appropriate that scientists should raise concerns about these trends, keep a close eye on them, and endeavor to learn as much about them as possible. But all of the evidence to date suggests that mankind's impact on Mother Nature is much less than we feared, and global warming, if it exists, may be a natural phenomenon beyond our ability to control.

In any event, there is a great diversity of opinion among scientists regarding the true nature of global warming and to what extent man-made chemicals are a factor. However, there is no diversity of opinion among economists about what would happen if we were to embrace the radical prescriptions of the environmental extremists who would have us simply shut down our industrial complex and mothball internal combustion vehicles in homage to their theory.

"People sometimes object that it's immoral to put a price tag on human health," the *Washington Post* opined, but given the vast expenditures required to abate pollution, "surely it makes sense to do the kind of analysis that weighs one health threat against another and shows where reductions in pollution will pay off most effectively in lower rates of illness and death."

The *Post*'s comments reflect a welcome coming-of-age among the major news media regarding the frequent excesses and irrationalities of the environmental movement, and an awakening long overdue. For more years than I care to recall, the media have served as a willing accessory in fomenting environmental hysteria. Branding this unhappy situation journalistic "error on a grand scale," former *Post* ombudsman Richard Harwood wrote in 1991 that media complicity in "environmental nondisasters such as Three Mile Island, Love Canal, Agent Orange, and the multimillion dollar asbestos removal scam" is rarely confessed.

The EPA's own Scientific Advisory Board concluded in 1990 that environmental laws "are more reflective of public perceptions of risk than of scientific understanding of risk." Former EPA administrator William Reilly said, "What we have had in the U.S. is environmental agenda setting by episodic panic." "We in the media bear a key share of the responsibility," wrote Hodding Carter III. "Our habits, our forms, and our attitudes almost guarantee that the shadows on the wall are far more important than the real-world life they represent."

In early 1993, the *New York Times* ran a series of four hard-hitting articles, prominent on the front page, acknowledging many of the wasteful follies carried out in the name of environmentalism.

A few weeks later, the *Washington Post* weighed in with an in-depth analysis of the global warming scenario, also on its front page, adding a dose of badly needed reality to the dire warnings emanating from the environmentalist camp.

THE WORST POLLUTION

In central Africa, young people frequently die before their sixteenth birthday from dysentery that they get from organisms in the putrid water they are obliged to bathe in and cook with. In parts of eastern Europe the landscape resembles the moon, except that the moon is not littered with cesspools of deadly chemical wastes and other industrial effluents. In the major cities of India, the gutters carry raw sewage among the people walking to and fro on their daily business.

The most threatening form of pollution known to human-kind is poverty. Wherever poverty prevails, the environment is a mess. Before there can be any serious attempt to clean up man-made impurities and restore nature's delicate balance, there must first be sufficient wealth to pay the cost without depriving people of their basic needs, among which is the opportunity to make a better future for themselves and their children. To the extent environmental controls undermine our economic base, they threaten our ability to pursue the environmental goals we all share.

One of the most destructive aspects of the EPA's command and control approach to environmental regulation is that it stifles innovation and creativity. There is no opportunity, much less reward, for finding better, more efficient, and more cost-effective ways to achieve desired ends. The long-term impact of such an approach can only be to reduce our competitiveness and erode our economic position.

The EPA's counterproductive emphasis on command and control is itself driven by the "good guys versus bad guys" mentality that characterizes many environmental groups and more than a few EPA bureaucrats. It is a form of childishness our society can no longer afford to indulge. I never cease to be amazed by casual references by environmentalists to "anti-environmental" forces seeking to subvert their noble cause. I have often wondered what real antienvironmentalism would be like. Would an antienvironmentalist rise in the morning, take a whiff of fresh air, and lament the absence of gritty smog? Or would he perhaps look upon a clear mountain stream and complain about the absence of raw sewage or industrial effluents? Is it really possible for any rational person to be antienvironment?

I don't think so. I believe the existence of "antienvironmentalism" is, like so many alleged environmental hazards, a figment of the fevered imagination of a few zealots who have permitted their fanaticism to subvert their thought processes. We are all environmentalists who treasure Mother Nature and desire to live in harmony with natural forces. The business community has done more than any other sector of society to translate this vision into reality and continues to do more. That is not at issue.

Environmental legislation poses the largest major impediment to meaningful regulatory reform if only because it involves so many distinct regulatory laws that must be reconsidered and amended one at a time. Each needs a rich infusion of common sense, which requires convincing proof of real hazards before regulations are issued and then a no-nonsense cost-benefit analysis to establish that the benefits of every regulation are commensurate with the costs. The EPA must be required to address the issue of scientific integrity and its institutional reluctance to acknowledge major mistakes—such as the asbestos hoax and the false report on secondary cigarette smoke.

A separate issue is that of false claims of environmental hazards that are embraced by the news media and used to provoke public hysteria, often with calamitous results. Perhaps it is not reasonable to expect news reporters to sort fact from fiction when complex environmental issues are at stake. There should be at least one respectable organization with environmental expertise that the media could call upon to review claims made by environmental groups and to quickly douse inflammatory reports that have little basis in fact. The EPA would be the obvious candidate for this job, but its record in this regard does not inspire confidence.

The compelling challenge is to achieve the best environmental result for the least cost and to focus our limited resources on real dangers instead of imaginary ones.

LAYING DOWN THE LAW
TO LAWYERS

The law's final justification is in the good it does or fails to do to the society of a given place and time. —ALBERT CAMUS

In 1983, Merrell Dow, a leading pharmaceutical company, withdrew its antinausea drug for pregnant women, Bendectin, from the market. Though doctors deemed it safe and no ill effects of the drug were proven, several mothers of children with birth defects had assumed a connection and sued the company. Merrell Dow finally decided the cost of defending itself outweighed the revenue produced by sales of the drug.

The following year, a woman named Karen Bilbray, who had depended upon Bendectin to get her safely through two prior pregnancies, went into shock without it and almost died. Bilbray's husband, Representative Brian Bilbray, Republican from California, attributes the premature death of their child born from that pregnancy to the trauma his wife went through when—because of the threat of lawsuits—she could not get Bendectin.

In 1988, Rawlings Sporting Goods decided to stop manufacturing or selling football helmets. Rawlings became the eighteenth U.S. manufacturer in as many years to abandon that once profitable product line. According to Riddell, one of the few helmet manufacturers left in the United States, half of the cost of a football helmet goes to liability-related expenses.

In Europe, Volvo has offered built-in child safety seats in its vehicles for more than a decade, but it does not include them in the cars it sells in America. Cars sold in the United States are not required to have child safety seats, but once a manufacturer installs one it becomes legally responsible for its performance under all circumstances.

And who can forget the stunning saga of eighty-one-year-old Stella Liebeck of Albuquerque, New Mexico, who spilled a cup of scalding hot coffee on herself and sued McDonald's for selling it to her, winning a judgment of $2.9 million (which later was reduced substantially). Ms. Liebeck is indignant that her case is being used as an example of legal excess. In her view, she deserved compensation because McDonald's coffee is unusually hot and her injury was truly severe.

But the extent of Ms. Liebeck's injury is not the issue. Rather, it is her complicity in spilling hot coffee on herself, holding someone else responsible, and using the legal system to translate her accidental injury into a successful raid on a business bank account. Reasonable people are asking if this is fair or serves any viable social or economic purpose.

Ms. Liebeck's award was not an aberration but rather one more chapter in a continuing saga of increasingly zany legal judgments. We are as a nation on a litigation binge. Many otherwise sensible citizens have come to view our legal system as a giant lottery in which any real or imagined injury can be a ticket to windfall profits.

In *The Liability Maze*, Peter Huber and Robert Litan put the annual price tag for litigation in our society at $80 billion to $180 billion, a large gap reflecting the difficulty of assessing the total impact of lawsuits. A prominent actuarial consulting firm, Tillinghast, Nelson & Warren, Inc., estimated the direct cost of the tort component of the civil justice system to be $132 billion in 1991. That is 60 percent of what we spend on education from kindergarten through the twelfth grade and two and one-half times what we spend on police and fire protection nationwide.

One statistic that is relatively easy to identify is the increase of lawsuits. Case filings in federal court increased over 1,100 percent between 1974 and 1990, rising from 1,579 to more than 18,000. The action in state courts is even more awesome. In 1990, there were more than 100 million lawsuits filed at the state level. These are large numbers that may not by themselves prove the existence of a lawsuit epidemic, but they justify a rigorous examination of and public debate about a system that plays a vital role in our society and economy.

The United States enjoys the dubious distinction of being the lawsuit capital of the world because with only 5 percent of the world's people we employ about 70 percent of the world's attorneys. Of course, there are some practical reasons why this nation has a greater commitment to law than other nations do. Hundreds of millions of diverse Americans from a variety of backgrounds and cultures are engaged in a variety of commercial and social activities that often lead to disputes. We are able to get along as peacefully and efficiently as we do in large part because we have a ubiquitous legal apparatus to help resolve quarrels and atone for injustice. Many disputes that could lead to violence are peacefully resolved in our courts. Thus, it is rather simplistic to compare our legal system with others such as Japan's, in which a virtually homogenous people share an ancient bias against confrontation and disputes.

Further, given our unique reliance on law to keep our diverse society and complex economy operating smoothly, it stands to reason our legal system will produce some bizarre results. Anecdotes of apparently irrational legal decisions, such as Ms. Liebeck's coffee judgment, do not in and of themselves bespeak a legal system gone haywire. Anyone can have a bad day.

But the evidence of a lawsuit epidemic in this country, like the evidence of a regulation epidemic, is more than anecdotal. Indeed, there is increasingly persuasive data to suggest the growing cost of our legal system, and its detrimental impact on our economy, is far out of proportion to its utility. Those who would dismiss the lawsuit epidemic as a myth or fabrication are challenging a reality that has become a daily fact of life to most Americans. Anecdotes of legal excess reflect the world we see around us and add a human dimension to an otherwise arcane issue.

A CHILLING EFFECT

Perhaps the most destructive impact of the lawsuit epidemic, stated in human terms, is not the money spent on litigation and awards but the chilling effect the threat of litigation has on business decisions, discouraging introduction of new products, construction of new businesses, and creation of new jobs.

Because litigation is only one of many obstacles business must contend with, it is often difficult to isolate and measure its direct impact on business decisions. Nevertheless, litigation and the threat of litigation emerge time and again as priority reasons for critical business decisions. A survey by The Conference Board reported that due to liability concerns, 47 percent of U.S. manufacturers have withdrawn products from the market, 39 percent have decided not to introduce new product lines, 25 percent have discontinued some forms of product research, about 15 percent have laid off workers as a direct result of product liability problems, and 8 percent have actually closed plants.

The actual number of lawsuits does not tell the full story, nor would accurate data on out-of-court settlements forced by threat of large judgments if such data were available. (Many settlements, including Ms. Liebeck's, are kept confidential.) The most profound and lasting damage wrought by excessive litigation is the chilling effect it has on innovation and discovery. "Scientific inquiry is stifled," Malcolm Skolnick, a professor of biophysics at the University of Texas who is also a lawyer, told the House Commerce Committee. "Ideas in areas where litigation has occurred will not receive support for exploration and development. Producers fearful of possible suit will discourage additional investigation which can be used against them in future claims."

Similarly, our open-ended liability system puts American business at a decided disadvantage in competition with foreign nations that do not permit their attorneys to plunder their engines of economic growth like we do. For example, Puritan-Bennett, a major domestic manufacturer of hospital equipment, stopped making anesthesia gas machines because of rising liability costs. Today, two foreign manufacturers dominate a U.S. market once filled by a half dozen eager domestic competitors.

The United States has far and away the most permissive product liability rules in the world, and our competitors routinely take advantage of this. If an American product sold abroad malfunctions, contributing to injury or loss, the owner can sue in the United States, with reasonable prospect of a generous judgment. Such suits are almost unheard of in Japan, as are large judgments. The Japanese people recognize the value of business ventures to their society and are reluctant to see them plundered.

As for our competitors in Europe, the European Communities Directive does not allow for liability if the manufacturer was in compliance with the mandates of public authorities, if existing technology did not reveal the existence of a flaw, or if a capital good involved in the case was more than fifteen years old. That fifteen-year rule makes U.S. corporate leaders envious, for here they are held accountable for one-hundred-year-old capital products even when they have been altered or modified by subsequent users without the manufacturer's knowledge or consent.

Also, while U.S. manufacturers must wrestle with fifty different state liability laws, our European competitors need trouble themselves with only that one simple EC directive. Even worse is the specter of punitive damages, a unique American invention in which the defendant is required to pay not only the actual costs associated with personal injury or property damage but also punitive damages as a deterrent. Punitive damage awards often run into the millions of dollars, sometimes hundreds of millions.

United States Supreme Court Justice Sandra Day O'Connor has observed that "The frequency and size of [punitive damage] awards have been skyrocketing," and that the "upward trajectory continues unabated" without "a corresponding expansion of procedural protections or predictability."

In a 1991 report, the President's Council on Competitiveness cited a Department of Commerce study that found that our foreign competitors often enjoy product liability insurance costs twenty to fifty times lower than U.S. firms. The Council found also that the estimated cost of product liability suits in the United States is equal to the combined profits of the nation's two hundred largest corporations.

STRANGLING INNOVATION

Potential liability has become an integral part of every business decision, including whether or not to launch new businesses or product lines, and for good reason. A representative of the nation's machine tool industry testified before the House Commerce Committee in 1990 that it spends seven times more on product liability insurance than on research and development. According to a study by the Rand Institute for Civil Justice, 87 percent of American companies will become defendants in a product liability claim at least once. Stories of promising new products that never make it to market because of potential liability are as common as lawyer jokes but not nearly as funny.

For example, Unison Industries kept an advanced electronic ignition system for light aircraft off the market; Union Carbide dropped development of a suitcase-size kidney dialysis unit; Monsanto canceled introduction of a biodegradable asbestos substitute; and—according to *Science* magazine—many pharmaceutical firms have abandoned promising research for an AIDS vaccine. In fact, Dr. Jonas Salk, who discovered the polio vaccine a generation ago, admitted before his death in 1995 that even if he succeeded in developing an AIDS vaccine, he didn't know of any U.S. manufacturer that would produce it—because of potential liability.

The devastating impact of the lawsuit epidemic on medical research and practice is perhaps the clearest and most damning evidence that something is amiss, if only because the cause-and-effect relationship is so clear and because the impact on people is unambiguous. The Bendectin that might have saved Representative Bilbray's child is as safe as any medicine can be. It was approved by the Food and Drug Administration and enjoyed a sterling reputation among health professionals.

But every lawsuit, however misguided, must be defended at

great cost and in danger of a large judgment, despite evidence of a product's safety. As McDonald's discovered in Stella Liebeck's suit, juries don't always return predictable verdicts.

What's missing from all this is a commonsense understanding that where medicine is practiced there will always be unfortunate outcomes and not every one justifies a lawsuit and damages. To many attorneys, however, any unsuccessful medical treatment can be a cause for action. Where people have suffered injury and corporate spokesmen appear to be callous or indifferent, there is a tendency among some jurors to make the business pay, if only because they know the business has money and the injured plaintiff, as culpable as he or she may be, does not.

What the jurors fail to understand is that their heartfelt sympathies are being expressed at great cost, and not just to the businesses they rule against. "Innovative new products are not being developed or are being withheld from the market because of liability concerns," the American Medical Association said. "Certain older technologies have been removed from the market, not because of sound scientific evidence indicating lack of safety or efficacy, but because product liability suits have exposed manufacturers to unacceptable financial risks."

Americans now depend on single companies to supply vaccines for polio, measles, mumps, rubella, and rabies. Lederle Laboratories, the lone maker of the diphtheria, pertussis, and tetanus (DPT) vaccine, raised its price per dose from $2.80 to $11.40 in 1987 to cover the price of lawsuits. As former Vice President Dan Quayle observed, the hepatitis B vaccine costs $160 here and only $12 in Taiwan because of the cost of U.S. product liability laws.

DEFENSIVE MEDICINE

Another adverse result of excessive litigation is defensive medicine. There are more than nine hundred new malpractice lawsuits filed in this country every working day, and the average award involves about $300,000. The annual tab for direct medical liability costs is about $7 billion, but indirect costs are much greater. The ever present threat of malpractice lawsuits forces doctors to prescribe many expensive tests and procedures that are legally necessary for the physicians, not medically necessary for the patients.

A study by the American Medical Association found that 66 percent of doctors admit they order more diagnostic tests, 54 percent schedule more follow-up visits, and 70 percent order more consultations because of liability concerns. A survey by *Medical Economics* revealed that 26 percent of physicians waste more than $50,000 a year on defensive medicine, and 14 percent waste more than $100,000 a year. Thus, every year the nation's medical bill is increased by as much as $40 billion by unnecessary procedures to avoid potential litigation.

Even more chilling is the increasing scarcity of critical medical specialties. In many parts of the country it is becoming more and more difficult to find doctors willing to provide obstetrical services to high-risk women because of potential liability. A survey of obstetricians found that 70 percent had a claim filed against them, generally for babies born with birth defects, most of which had nothing to do with the quality of medical treatment.

It is not rational to suppose that obstetricians are less competent today than they were ten or twenty years ago, or less committed to their patients. To the contrary, all evidence points to a profession constantly reaching new peaks of proficiency and ability as researchers discover new therapies and techniques. But the most immediate result of this progress in obstetrics is to preserve the lives of many babies who would not have survived in earlier years, and many of these come into the world with a variety of birth defects. Unfortunately, the first impulse of the parents caught in this tragic situation is to sue their doctors.

Then again, perhaps it isn't a natural impulse at all. Maybe there's another reason, such as a surplus of lawyers looking for an easy score.

A LAWYER GLUT

In the past two decades, the number of practicing attorneys in the United States has doubled to more than 866,000. The *average* income of members of the America Bar Association is $103,800 and their average household income is $158,400.

It is impossible to tell if young people are motivated to enroll in law school by a yearning to pursue justice, but it is clear money has become the consuming objective of many practicing attorneys to the exclusion of higher ideals. In 1989, *Forbes* magazine published a report asserting the nation's top 134 lawyers together raked in some $860 million in one year. That's right up there with baseball players, movie stars, and rock bands—only lawyers are not so entertaining.

The sheer abundance of lawyers tends to promote excessive litigation. From 1980 to 1989 auto accident rates fell and the number of property damage claims filed per million miles driven also fell, by 12 percent. Because cars became steadily safer during that period, personal injury claims should have fallen even faster than property damage claims, but instead they rose by 15 percent.

Perhaps this was because automobiles cannot sue for pain and suffering, no matter how severe their injury. In Philadelphia, where many aggressive attorneys work, there were seventy-five bodily injury claims for every one hundred claims of damage to cars—compared to only sixteen per hundred in Pittsburgh.

Of course, criticism of lawyers is nothing new. "Woe to ye

also ye lawyers," said Jesus of Nazareth, "for ye lade men with burdens grievous to be borne, while ye yourselves touch not the burdens with one of your fingers." "The first thing we do, let's kill all the lawyers," wrote Shakespeare. "Why does a hearse horse snicker," wrote poet Carl Sandburg, "hauling a lawyer away?"

A few years ago, I scored some serious laughs with a tongue-in-cheek proposal to swap lawyers to Japan for Toyotas. I wasn't sure if more Toyotas in the United States would help us become more competitive, but I had no doubt a few ship-loads of American lawyers would undermine Japan's economy in no time—to our advantage. They would be filing lawsuits left and right, taking business to the cleaners, and draining capital from productive enterprises like they do here.

But behind the laughs lies an increasingly depressing specta-cle of honorable professionals in denial, refusing to acknowl-edge the conspicuous avarice among their own ranks or the pressing need for a serious housecleaning and reassessment of their proper role in a modern society. One looks in vain for any evidence of soul-searching among the legal clan. Indeed, if there is one singular trait that distinguishes the legal profes-sion in America today it must surely be an inability to be em-barrassed.

A 1995 poll by *U.S. News & World Report* revealed that 69 percent of Americans believe lawyers are only sometimes hon-est or not usually honest. To suggest that people are only hon-est part of the time, such as when there is no temptation to be dishonest, is a damning comment on their character. Perhaps more significant, 56 percent of respondents said lawyers use the system to protect the powerful and enrich themselves. Ac-cording to law professor Lester Brickman of the Benjamin N. Cardozo School of Law in New York, Americans are con-cerned that lawyers have far too much influence in our society and that they commit "enormous amounts of outright fraud."

In California, the lawyers for Rodney King, the guy whose beating by Los Angeles police was secretly videotaped, billed the city for $4.4 million in fees for representing an indigent, including charges for appearing in the media and going to King's birthday party. A judge later reduced the bill to "only" $1.6 million, but that is $1.6 million out of the taxpayers' pockets.

An article in the January 30, 1995, *U.S. News & World Report* recited a litany of abuses by lawyers that have become all too common: "Consider, for example, the law firm in a major bankruptcy case that billed its bankrupt client $177,844 for the time it spent preparing the bill. Or the attorney who drafted a legal motion that applied to thousands of separate cases that his client, an insurer, faced in a huge asbestos litigation—and then billed the clients as many as three thousand separate times for the same twelve minutes of his time. Or the Denver firm that proudly claimed its lawyers didn't fly first class, until an auditor hired by one client found that although the firm bought business-class tickets for its attorneys, the lawyers simply were upgrading their tickets to first class at the airport—and passing the charge on to clients."

Bill padding has become so endemic to legal practice that it is generally regarded as a joke. One law firm auditor quoted in *U.S. News* said he found overcharges in 90 percent of the cases he is hired to examine.

DEEP POCKETS

But perhaps no single issue speaks more loudly and convincingly about legal avarice than the concept of joint and several liability, or the "deep pockets" doctrine. This curious concept of justice holds that any company or person held partially responsible for an injury or harm can be held fully responsible for the judgment if it is the only defendant wealthy enough to pay the judgment. The very idea that guilt and responsibility are directly proportional to one's bank account is one that only lawyers could have conceived and put into practice.

The effect of this doctrine is at times almost too bizarre to believe. For example, the Gates Corporation, a tire and rubber manufacturer in Denver, Colorado, is one of forty-five defendants being sued for the fire at a chicken processing plant in North Carolina in 1991 that killed twenty-five people. The actual responsibility for that tragedy was not difficult to ascertain. There was no fire alarm or sprinkler system in the plant, and the exits were locked. But the owner of that plant has no money.

Gates Corporation, on the other hand, is a profitable company with assets. And under what pretext, you may ask, is Gates being sued? Well, Gates made the rubber hoses and some other products used in the plant, which allegedly contributed to the toxic fumes that were so deadly in that fiery hell. For this reason and no other, Gates is spending huge amounts of money to defend itself from a potentially catastrophic judgment.

Nor is this an isolated event. Gates Corporation spends $3.5 million a year defending itself against suits with no more merit than that one—as when failure of one of its fan belts is blamed for a car wreck. The problem for Gates is greatly aggravated by the legal presumption that the plaintiff doesn't have to prove Gates is guilty. Rather, Gates must prove it is innocent. And proving a negative, as every logician knows, is virtually impossible.

Gates Corporation vice president Thomas J. Gibson says the company often has to make purely economic decisions whether to pay a $100,000 settlement or spend $500,000 in legal fees to avoid it, risking an even larger loss. Whether or not the company actually did anything wrong or whether one of its products was actually defective is beside the point. "It's extortion, but we've had cases where we've felt that's the better way to go," Gibson said. "I cringe when I sign the checks."

The term "extortion" is used also by James Kimsey, chairman of America Online, Inc., who says that all high technology firms such as his are especially susceptible to legal action. They are frequently forced to defend and settle frivolous class-action suits at enormous cost in time and money "even though you have done nothing wrong, even though there is no merit to the suit—and that amounts to corporate extortion." Major universities have testified before Congress that they are reluctant to award research grants to small companies because, in the event of a lawsuit, the university would be viewed as the "deep pocket."

Consider the case of Dixie Flag Manufacturing Company of San Antonio, Texas, which learned the hard way how our corrupt legal system exploits small business. Dixie employs sixty-three people making American flags for businesses and classrooms across the country, from the little handheld flaglets to a huge 55-by-110-foot edition.

In 1991, the company was named in a suit filed by a man who claimed that while helping to lower a large flag, a powerful gust of wind billowed the flag and lifted him high into the air, causing him injuries. In the suit, the plaintiff alleged that the American flag was an "unreasonably dangerous product" that should be required to have warning labels on it.

The truly crazy thing about this story is that Dixie Flag did not make the flag involved in the incident and otherwise had no relationship with the incident or the people involved. But the company that had actually made and sold the flag was a one-man operation with no resources. Thus, the "deep pocket" legal doctrine of joint and several liability kicked in, making companies such as Dixie Flag liable. Dixie Flag's insurance company, against Dixie's wishes, eventually settled for $6,000. Two other flag makers, neither of which had anything to do with the accident, settled out of court for $14,000 and $1,500 respectively. In other words, the plaintiff managed to extort at least $21,500 from three companies that had nothing to do with the alleged injury without even having to establish in a court that there was in fact an injury.

SIZE IS NO DEFENSE

The size of the company, or extent of its legal resources, offers it no immunity from such legal plundering. Perhaps no other recent legal action underscores more dramatically how haywire our legal system has become, or the devastating destruction it causes, than the much ballyhooed controversy over breast implants.

It all began in 1992 when Dr. David Kessler, administrator of the Food and Drug Administration, decided to ban silicone gel–filled breast implants because, he explained, the manufacturers had not demonstrated their safety. Such implants had been available for thirty years and approximately 1 percent of American women have had them, often for reconstruction after mastectomy for breast cancer. At the time Kessler issued the ban there had been no systematic studies of the effects of breast implants, and thus there was zero scientific evidence to confirm a hazard associated with them.

The only thing known for certain was that there could be complications associated with the surgery required to insert breast implants, as with any surgery. Other alleged ill effects of breast implants, such as a purported association with connective tissue disease, were nothing more than rumors and suspicions. But the absence of scientific evidence against breast implants did not deter Dr. Kessler from his rash action and had even less impact on the hordes of attorneys who rushed to cash in on the action. In the two years following the FDA ban, more than a thousand lawyers filed more than

16,000 lawsuits on behalf of women with breast implants. Though still maintaining its innocence and the safety of breast implants, the primary manufacturer, Dow Corning, had to declare bankruptcy.

This decision is especially galling because the company had already agreed to pay $2 billion of a $4.25 billion overall settlement. But a federal judge wanted the class action award renegotiated upward, and while the lawyers involved already were guaranteed 25 percent of the settlement, they wanted even more. Some seven thousand plaintiffs opted out of the initial settlement in order to sue Dow Corning in separate cases. There was no way the company could contend with such an avalanche of litigation, so it had no choice but to seek protection under Chapter 11.

This outrage against common sense and decency will harm every citizen because Dow Corning makes 80 percent of the silicone used in heart valves, pacemakers, and other medical devices and will now probably abandon the business altogether.

Meanwhile, two years after breast implants were taken off the market, and two months after the class action settlement was announced, the first study of a possible link between breast implants and connective tissue disease was published, and it found no link. The respected Mayo Clinic compared a group of 749 women who had received breast implants between 1964 and 1991 with 1,498 of their neighbors matched for age. The results showed clearly that the group with implants was no more likely to develop connective disease or related symptoms than the group without implants.

Other studies of larger groups have reinforced that initial finding. Whatever else one may think about the cultural significance of breast implants, there is not now—nor has there ever been—credible scientific evidence that they present a serious health threat to women who have them. And yet the legal system has permitted a group of rapacious attorneys to push that reality to the side as if it simply didn't matter while they plundered one of our most vigorous and vital corporations into bankruptcy. The purpose and effect of this atrocity was not to protect women from a hazard, because there is no hazard, or to provide financial relief to victims of corporate malfeasance, for there are neither victims nor malfeasance in evidence. It was nothing more or less than a demonstration of the power of unscrupulous lawyers to plunder our economic system for their own financial benefit and for no other purpose.

GREED

The self-enrichment of attorneys is and remains the driving force behind this avalanche of increasingly meritless lawsuits. A substantial percentage of these lawsuits are brought by attorneys working on a contingency fee basis. That means the plaintiffs do not have to put money up to pay for the legal work involved; the attorneys take the risk of their time and effort and get nothing if the case is lost.

But if the case is won or, more likely, a settlement is reached, the attorneys walk off with a large chunk of money. The size of that chunk can vary widely but generally ranges between a third and a half of the settlement or judgment. Joseph DelFico, director of income security issues for the General Accounting Office (GAO), said a 1989 GAO study revealed that more than half of a defendant's payment in product liability cases goes to attorneys. If the case is appealed, the attorney's payout can double.

A study by the management firm of Towers Perrin found that the U.S. tort system returns less than 50 cents on the dollar to people it is designed to help, and returns less than 25 cents on the dollar to compensate for actual economic losses.

In asbestos cases, after attorneys and expert witnesses are

paid, the plaintiffs are generally lucky to get one-third of the money paid by the defendant. The Rand Corporation reported that 70 cents of every dollar awarded in asbestos cases in the 1980s was paid to lawyers. Peter Angelos, owner of the Baltimore Orioles, acquired most of his considerable fortune via his share of a $225 million fee for a single lawsuit against asbestos manufacturers.

Lawyers claim the contingency system is fair because they take all the risk and get nothing if they lose. But according to Cardozo's Lester Brickman, in upward of a third of all contingency cases, the contingency is in name only.

Where liability is not at issue and there is no chance a case will go to trial, a contingency fee amounts to a scam. The lawyer is deceiving the client and absconding with an unearned share of the plaintiff's judgment or award.

Brickman cited as an example the 1989 crash of a Coca-Cola truck into a school bus in Alton, Texas, in which twenty-one children were killed and another sixty injured. Brickman estimated that the lawyers who represented the plaintiffs on a contingency fee basis walked off with $30,000 per hour for their labors. One waits for an outcry about such abuses from honest attorneys or an investigation by the local bar association. One waits in vain.

RIPPING OFF CONSUMERS

A 1992 study by the Rand Corporation calculated that "business will spend a minimum of $31 million on noncleanup Superfund activities, primarily legal fees, over the next thirty years." This was not what Congress had in mind when it passed Superfund, nor what the citizens wanted when they expressed support for cleanup of potentially hazardous waste disposal sites. But the lawyers have once again stolen the show to their own advantage—and to the disadvantage of the rest of us.

The ultimate indictment of our legal system is not that occasional outrages occur or that a lot of lawsuits are filed or that business pays out a lot of money in legal fees, judgments, and settlements. Rather, it is in the fact that after all is said and done, the legal system is enriching itself at the expense of the people, making our economy less competitive, destroying jobs, and strangling opportunities.

Plaintiffs' lawyers contend that punitive damages are awarded in only a handful of cases and that the more notorious excesses, such as Stella Liebeck's suit against McDonald's, are usually reduced on appeal. This is all quite true and irrelevant. The same statistics also confirm that 95 percent of defective-product and personal injury cases are settled out of court and are not subject to appeal. Punitive damages are almost always sought in these cases, and the possibility of huge awards serves to drive more generous settlements.

Thus, businesses such as the Gates Corporation in Denver find themselves paying out huge awards when they are in the right because they cannot afford the cost of litigation plus the possibility of incurring huge punitive damages.

A review of 30,000 patient records in New York found 280 instances of injuries caused by negligence. In all, 47 people filed malpractice suits, but those 47 included only 8 who were among the actual victims of negligence. Of the remaining 39, 12 had no injuries at all and the others had experienced some sort of "adverse event," but not because of negligence.

Lawyers insist the right to sue is the last guarantee of consumer rights, a constant reminder to business to provide safe and healthful products. But there is rarely any direct correlation between defective products and liability awards. Yale Law professor George Priest has said that "though the annual numbers of tort suits and liability insurance premiums rose sharply during the 1980s, injury rates for consumers and workers, death rates from medical procedures, and aviation accident rates declined no faster than they had been in the 1970s when premium costs and the volume of tort suits was much lower."

A study by the Brookings Institution found that, far from ensuring safer products, lawsuits discourage many safety improvements—such as Volvo's built-in child safety seat. Our legal system regards any improvement in safety as evidence that the earlier product was unsafe, and thus as cause for legal action. Therefore, it effectively discourages safety innovations.

Consumer advocate Ralph Nader wrote to me recently to urge I abandon my advocacy of legal reforms. The first part of his letter described the alleged human carnage occurring in America because of callous and indifferent corporations producing unsafe products. The second part explained that we needed to keep our present system intact in order to deter such abuses. I was left to wonder why, if our legal system is so effective in deterring abuses, we still have all that human carnage Ralph was complaining about. In any event, there is no epidemic of human carnage in America due to unsafe products and services. To the contrary, the average lifespan of Americans increases every year because we live in a healthful environment and have access to the safest food, consumer products, and medicines in the world.

In 1995, the business community—spearheaded by the U.S. Chamber of Commerce—finally got a serious federal product liability law approved by Congress. Without question, this achievement, coming as it did after eighteen years of futile effort, was made possible by the small business contingent in the 104th Congress. It was long overdue.

Unfortunately, the clout of the trial lawyers is such that a more comprehensive legal reform bill approved by the House never had a chance in the Senate. The product liability bill was a breakthrough, but it is only part of what we need. To impose some rationality on our legal system we need to enact strict limits on punitive damage awards, abolish the outrageous doctrine of joint and several liability, and curb the practice of contingency fees. The runaway litigiousness that so beguiles Ralph Nader and trial attorneys does not serve the interests of consumers and workers. To the contrary, it drives up consumer prices, discourages introduction of safety innovations, and keeps promising medicines off the market. To small businesses the threat of spurious lawsuits is an ever present sword of Damocles hanging over their heads that could fall at any moment, in effect committing unprovoked murder of a going enterprise and the dream that inspired it.

DISCOURAGED
EMPLOYERS

*My father taught me to work. He did not teach
me to like it.* —ABRAHAM LINCOLN

N ear the front door of a machine shop in the suburbs of
a major eastern city sits a conspicuous metal stamping
machine replete with the latest safety features, guards, auto-
matic shutoffs, and various other accoutrements designed by
well-meaning safety engineers to ensure the operator returns
home at night with the same number of limbs and digits as
when the day began. The machine is several years old but still
looks new because it is rarely used. The machinists view it—
just as an Indy 500 driver might view a go-cart or a jet pilot a
small prop plane—as an insult to their prowess. The proprietors of the small business regard the machine with even more
contempt because they invested a substantial amount of
money in what amounts to a dead loss. All of the safety fea-

tures render the machine extremely slow and unwieldy, virtually unusable in their high-paced work environment.

But the conspicuous apparatus, dubbed "the OSHA machine," serves a practical purpose. When the safety inspector comes to the door, the machine is quickly turned on. The well-rehearsed employees know their roles and pretend to be intently working with it. For as long as the OSHA inspection lasts, the performance is played out. If the inspection goes on long enough, they actually do some real work on the machine. After the inspector is gone they breathe a sigh of relief and return to their real work on the old, greasy machines in the rear of the shop.

To suggest the employers are indifferent to safety evokes laughter, for the employers work side by side with their employees and are just as exposed as they are to whatever risks attend their daily activities.

There are thirteen employees, sometimes fourteen when the work load grows especially heavy, but never fifteen. The proprietors—two middle-aged men—explain that they need more employees, but to hire the fifteenth employee would put them into an entirely new government bracket in which the OSHA inspector would be the least of their troubles. Some of the better-known federal statutes that kick in when a company reaches the fifteen-employee level are the Civil Rights Act of 1964, the Americans with Disabilities Act of 1990, and the Civil Rights Amendments of 1991. As the employment level rises above that, more and more laws kick in. The penalty imposed by big government for expansion in business is a growing burden of responsibility, paperwork and liability.

The proprietors have no desire to discriminate against anyone and in fact have several members of minority groups on their payroll. There are women performing administrative tasks in the office but none in the machine shop because the proprietors have yet to encounter any women eager to perform the hard, dirty work involved. There are no employees with serious disabilities on the payroll either, though with regard to that issue also they are open-minded. It would depend, they told me, on the reasonableness of any accommodations that would be required and whether the applicant could operate the equipment safely.

Of course, the proprietors could go out and beat the bushes searching for females and people with disabilities to learn the machinist trade, but they are struggling businesspeople with insufficient overhead and administrative staff to perform such tasks. Their days are more than full with trying to stay abreast of work demands, keeping the equipment in running order, ensuring their products meet strict quality standards, and making certain the money coming in exceeds the money going out. The penalty for failure is bankruptcy.

These businessmen are crusty, rough-edged fellows trying to survive in deadly earnest competition with companies much bigger than theirs. They shy away from the mind-numbing requirements that civil rights laws impose upon employers, including the awesome array of paperwork and virtually endless legal liability.

Large corporations endowed with in-house administrative staff and legal counsel can contend with Uncle Sam's paper chase but not entrepreneurs trying to run small machine shops. They lack the professional skills to do it themselves and cannot afford to hire lawyers to do it for them.

Thus, they deliberately keep their workforce small, even though it means they must turn down potentially profitable jobs when their personnel are stretched to the limit. To them, the government—with all of its incomprehensible rules, endless forms, and nitpicking demands—is a greater threat than Japanese or European competition. Uncle Sam is in a real and present sense their most dangerous enemy.

This situation is tragic because the work these fellows are

doing is on the cutting edge of the technological transformation of the modern industrial work place—employing the very kind of skills blue-collar workers must acquire if they are to maintain their toehold in the middle class. Those machines in the rear of their shop are not pleasant to look at—greasy behemoths looming above messy piles of metal shavings—but they are controlled by modern computers that enable them to produce efficiently finished products with extraordinary tolerances and exceptional quality. It would be in the interest of small businesses—and the nation—if such proprietors were bringing more employees on board and teaching them the refined job skills required in a high-tech industrial shop.

But the government, in pursuit of high-minded ideals, has created a bureaucratic monster before which small businesspeople flee in terror. When all of the red tape and paperwork and formal procedures are in place, it can take months to hire a new employee and years to get rid of one who doesn't work out, followed by the almost inevitable lawsuits. If the person discharged belongs to one or more of the officially protected groups—and most people belong to at least one of them—the business can look forward to charges of discrimination as well, with all of the investigations, reports, and litigation that entails. Uncle Sam has transformed the once simple act of hiring workers into a hazardous ordeal that, if mishandled, can literally destroy a productive enterprise. It is small wonder that many small business operations, such as the one I visited, deliberately remain small to avoid the red tape and unlimited risks associated with hiring.

The experience of those small business operators, shared with me in understandable confidentiality, is by no means unique. To the contrary, there is a mountain of evidence to suggest it represents a major trend in the nation's economy. A 1994 survey of two thousand manufacturing executives conducted by the National Association of Manufacturers found that 64.3 percent have delayed hiring specifically due to government mandates and regulations, 86.1 percent rely more on overtime and temporary help than five years ago due to government mandates and regulations, 84.6 percent of smaller companies deliberately keep their workforces small to avoid becoming subject to a variety of regulatory laws, and 50 percent of companies that could export are inhibited from trying to do so by the federal paperwork involved.

The latter item touches on what has become the most compelling labor issue of modern times—our competitiveness in the world marketplace and its impact on wage rates. Even when the economy is operating at full throttle and our basic export industries are flooding the world with made-in-the-USA products, there is still a growing sense of unease and anxiety about the future among our industrial workers. Secretary of Labor Robert Reich calls them "the anxious class" of workers, "most of whom hold jobs but who are justifiably uneasy about their own standing and fearful for their children's futures."

They have by no means lost the work ethic that sustained earlier generations of Americans. "A truly American sentiment recognizes the dignity of labor," said President Grover Cleveland, "and the fact that honor lies in honest toil." A century after Cleveland left office, the values he described remain intact. People still believe in the traditional work ethic and we are fortunate they do.

But while dignity and honor are wonderful things, they do not put food on the table or pay the rent. The American work ethic is perhaps the most valuable asset in our economic arsenal, but it is no longer enough. Many Americans who are eager and willing to work cannot find employment, and many who are employed find their wages are stranded in limbo, perhaps keeping pace with inflation, but just barely. They feel they are treading water, and they are losing the critical ability to hope for a better future for themselves and their children.

This is especially troubling to me because next to food and housing, I believe hope is the most essential ingredient of human happiness and social stability. Where hope dies, despair appears in its place. To a large extent, blue-collar working people are the heart and soul of the nation, and Secretary Reich is right—they indeed constitute "an anxious class."

THE DECLINE OF UNIONS

Once upon a time labor unions offered hope to despairing workers. Historically they achieved power by capitalizing on worker anger and anxiety and are trying to do the same today by responding to the frustrations of Reich's "anxious class." But the union message today is increasingly falling upon deaf ears.

The fatal flaw of contemporary American unionism is that it seizes power by capitalizing upon worker antipathy toward management and has no vision other than to continually fan the flames of worker discontent. The most benign efforts of management to modernize and improve the quality of work life are regarded as sinister efforts to undermine union influence. Unions devote most of their time and energy to campaigning for higher pay, more generous benefits, and restrictive work rules that make it ever more difficult for management to respond to new challenges and technologies.

The unions claim that contented, well-paid workers are an essential ingredient of productivity, and so they are. But beyond that it is difficult to identify any item on the union agenda that cannot fairly be viewed as a threat to productivity.

In any event, it is the union opposition to efficiency, not demands for money and benefits, that presents the greatest threat to progress. "Once 85 percent of national income goes to employees, the labor union has lost its original rationale, that of increasing the share of the national income that goes to the 'wage fund,' " writes consultant and author Peter Drucker. "After that all a labor union can do is increase the share of its members at the expense of other employees."

Most workers instinctively know this and, in most circumstances, take a dim view of union organizing efforts. Since 1955, when union strength was at its peak at 33.2 percent of the total workforce, union representation of workers has declined steadily to 15.5 percent. Take away the government sector, which represents virtually the only fertile ground for union organizing in recent years, and the percentage of remaining workers in the private, nonfarm sector who actually belong to unions is only 10.9 percent.

Those data bespeak a movement without a compelling product to sell. When a business experiences such a decline of market share, alarms go off. Top management is called on the carpet and given ultimatums. They must rethink their business and come up with a new approach. In recent years, some of the nation's premier corporations have gone through this painful process, and more than a few once powerful chief executive officers have been shown the door.

But the labor unions just keep on doing what they have always done—trying to foster antipathy between employers and employees and to take advantage of it. This approach is particularly ineffective with the small businesses that are today creating the lion's share of new jobs because most small business operators have a close rapport with their employees. Thus, year after year, working people turn a deaf ear to union entreaties. It is a worn-out song that few want to hear anymore.

Even in large work settings where workers are not earning enough to improve their economic situation, they still resist union organizing because they understand their dilemma is an outgrowth of changing technology for which unions have no solution. There was a time when any worker with minimal education and basic mechanical aptitude could look forward to a productive career on the factory floor, thanks in part to the influence of labor unions. When mass production was the driving force of American commerce, unionism helped workers obtain an equitable share of the economic pie and thus facilitated the evolution of a solid middle class among blue-collar workers. That in turn fostered ever bigger markets for U.S. manufacturing to serve. Whatever union strength survives today is based upon memory of that historic contribution.

But the world has changed, and with it the ability of unions to take advantage of worker angst. Commerce and industry are more splintered and diverse than a half century ago. Every day brings news of breathtaking progress in science and technology that is changing the way we work and live. The computer chip was a huge breakthrough, greater than the lightbulb, telephone, or internal combustion engine. Day by day it stalks through our economy flushing out fresh new ways to do things better and more efficiently—even in machine shops.

One effect of this sea change in the way the world works is the diminishing value of manual labor. Industry today needs workers who can think on their feet and relearn their jobs constantly. Tens of thousands of traditional industrial jobs are destroyed forever, but at the same time more high-tech jobs are being created in their place. A worker who is not mentally agile, who cannot adjust quickly to changing demands and who cannot help improve productivity is of marginal value to a business. Workers on the cutting edge of technology, however, are invaluable and have the power to displace their superiors who may lag in adapting to the rapid changes.

Data accumulated by the Bureau of Labor Statistics underscore this phenomenon. Between 1979 and 1993, a worker with a high school education lost 18.2 percent in real weekly earnings. During the same period, the average worker with a college education gained 5.2 percent. Stated another way, in 1979 a college-educated worker earned 49 percent more than a worker with only a high school education; by 1993 the college trained worker earned 83 percent more than the high school graduate.

The union quest to preserve the rights and prerogatives of unskilled labor are doomed to failure. When the workers are slow to grasp that reality, the results are often heartbreaking. For example, a few years ago my hometown of Chambersburg, Pennsylvania, underwent a grueling strike by the United Auto Workers Local 695 against T.B. Wood's Sons Company, a maker of electrical and mechanical power transmission products. The strike became a divisive issue in the community, turning neighbors against neighbors and even relatives against relatives.

It was clearly a case of workers trying to use union muscle to hold off reality. It didn't work. When the workers walked off the job, the company was suddenly freed to add new machinery, eliminate restrictive work rules, and foster a more cooperative work ethic. It quickly became more efficient and productive than it was before, while the displaced union workers watched their lives drift into bitterness, recrimination, and an inevitable decline in living standard.

Labor unions continue to wage these dismal quarrels against management with almost uniformly disastrous results for the workers and their communities. To the extent they set business free from union influence, as was the case at T.B. Wood's Sons Company, their best efforts benefit the corporations they strike against. Yet the unions continue the same obsolete approach day in and day out in a pathetic attempt to impose their outdated agenda on a world that has passed them by.

What the unions desperately need is a new vision of representing workers in a cooperative effort with management to achieve higher levels of efficiency, productivity, and profitability. "It is significant that in Japan trade unions are among the most vocal advocates of long-term investment strategies that emphasize productivity and growth," wrote Robert Reich in 1983 (some years before he became a union apologist as secretary of labor in the Clinton administration). The union movement in this country suffers from fossilized leadership trapped in a time warp. Until it inherits a new vision and embraces a more constructive agenda, it will continue to dissipate its energies in fruitless tribute to a bygone era.

The Malevolent Minimum

Whatever evils and misfortune labor unions neglect to inflict upon American workers are more than made up for by government interventions in the labor market that, more often than not, are driven by labor union pressure. Perhaps the most conspicuous example of this well-intentioned foolishness is the minimum wage.

If there was ever a time when the minimum wage served a viable purpose in our economy, it has long since passed. In the modern world, the free market needs no help from government in determining what a fair return on labor should be. Senator Ted Kennedy, Democrat from Massachusetts, and other advocates of the minimum wage, wax eloquent about the importance of rewarding work and how difficult it is for a family breadwinner to makes ends meet on the minimum wage. They neglect to add that raising the minimum wage by $1 or $2 per hour, or even $5 per hour, would not enable minimum wage workers to support families. The minimum wage is not, and was never intended to be, a basis for supporting families.

As originally conceived during the Great Depression, the

minimum wage was intended to prevent unscrupulous employers from taking advantage of hard times and exploiting desperate workers. But in the modern marketplace employers are competing in an open environment for skilled labor and lack coercive power to take advantage of people.

As a matter of fact, there is compelling evidence that raising the minimum wage can diminish the income level of poor families. "Predicated on the assumption that higher earnings translate into higher household resources," writes Carlos Bonilla of the Employment Policies Institute, "the minimum wage doctrine is totally at odds with the economic forces that define life for the lowest income segment of the working poor."

Bonilla believes that beneficiaries of a higher minimum wage not only have to pay higher taxes but also lose access to public assistance programs—such as Aid to Families with Dependent Children, Medicaid, and Food Stamps—which are reduced as a claimant's income rises. Since most antipoverty programs are partnerships between the federal and state governments, the impact of a higher minimum wage can vary.

For example, raising the minimum wage by $1 would reduce the annual resources of a single parent of one child in California by $1,800. A single parent with two or three children in California would lose $1 in income. That's a small loss but a loss nonetheless.

The typical minimum wage worker is a teenager from a middle-income family earning extra money for personal expenses. Such people tend to perform marginal tasks and to enter and leave the workforce at random intervals. A typical minimum wage job is as a clerk or short-order cook in a fast-food restaurant.

There are only 34,000 householders working full-time at the minimum wage who head families with incomes under $10,000 and another 24,000 such householders who work part-time. Altogether they represent less than 1 percent of all minimum wage workers, of whom there were about 4.7 million in 1994, with an additional 16.8 million workers earning between $4.25 and $6 per hour. The latter rate is equivalent to about half of the median earnings for all full-time workers.

Overall, in our labor force of about 127 million people, less than 4 percent are minimum wage workers and 17 percent can be described as low wage. Scarcely 2 percent of workers over thirty years old earn the minimum wage, and most of these are individuals in unusual circumstances for which no comprehensive government program would be relevant. Only .8 percent of all workers over forty work full-time at the minimum wage.

Furthermore, race is not a significant factor in the minimum wage calculation. Just over 81 percent of all minimum wage workers are white in a population that is 84 percent white overall.

In his 1995 State of the Union address, President Clinton called for a hike in the minimum wage to $5.15 per hour, a sharp 21 percent increase. In order to meet this increase in the cost of labor, which would serve primarily to endow middle-class kids with more recreation money, business, mainly small business, would have to fork over an additional $8 billion a year. That's enough to hire another 850,000 workers at the higher minimum wage.

But of course many of those small businesses could not afford the additional expense, and that is where the real downside of a higher minimum wage comes in. Every effort to raise the minimum wage evokes claims of job losses that, like anecdotes about regulatory excesses, are subject to debate. There is no way to apply a concrete number to it because the final impact would be measured in terms of tens of thousands of individual decisions by businesspeople, mostly small entrepreneurs, regarding whether to hire or fire, start up or shut down.

But there can be no doubt that a great many job opportunities would be lost, and almost all of them would be entry-level jobs for people with the fewest job skills who need opportunities the most. Several years ago the *New York Times* published an editorial stating that the appropriate minimum wage is "$0.00." That editorial reflected a realistic assessment of the dilemma created by any government-sanctioned attempt to regulate salaries. Many desperate kids aspire to enter the workforce but lack the most minimal understanding of how to acquire and keep a job. In many instances, their labor is not worth even today's minimum wage. Their best hope is to find an employer willing to pay them more than they are worth now in the hope they will blossom into useful workers later on. More than a few of us got our first work experience and learned positive work habits in this manner. But every increase in the minimum wage reduces the incentive for employers to take on marginal employees and hence reduces the opportunities for young people to acquire that all-important first work experience.

As a practical matter, the minimum wage is irrelevant to people at the bottom of the wage scale. As soon as an employee becomes useful and productive, the employer has incentive to raise his or her pay because a productive worker can easily find work elsewhere. The only beneficiaries of a higher minimum wage are unions that have escalators built into their contracts based upon the minimum wage and daffy politicians who mistake the minimum wage as a means of expressing their concern for society's down-and-out.

It is worth mentioning also that President Clinton had nothing to say about the minimum wage in his first two years of office, despite the urging of Secretary of Labor Robert Reich. He knew any such suggestion would be dead on arrival in Congress, even when the Democrats controlled both houses, because it is such a terrible idea. Only after the Republican landslide of 1994 did he bother to formally recommend an increase. It was not a serious proposal but rather a political stunt designed to generate publicity, make the opposition seem indifferent to the welfare of working people, and placate Clinton's restless friends in the labor union movement.

BIG BROTHER AT LARGE

In the spring of 1994, Secretary of Labor Robert Reich—who had earlier in his career spoken so benignly of the need for greater labor-management cooperation—personally appeared at the Dayton Tire Company in Oklahoma to announce a $7.5 million penalty for violations of the Occupational Safety and Health Act and later followed up with a court order shutting the plant down and putting eleven hundred Oklahomans out of work. Reich did not inform the company he was coming, although the international president of the union was notified well ahead of time and was on hand for the show. And that is exactly what it was—a show of solidarity between the Clinton administration and organized labor. In requesting the restraining order from the U.S. District Court, which shut down the plant, Reich's Labor Department claimed conditions in the plant constituted an "imminent danger" to employees.

But the original OSHA inspection that first revealed the alleged "imminent danger" had been conducted six months before Reich showed up on the site, and it is truly an extraordinary "imminent danger" that can simmer that long without causing real harm to someone. The following day, after the federal judge had a long look at the facts, he lifted the restraining order and the plant reopened.

But not before Reich held a press conference to warn that "American workers are not going to be sacrificed on the altar of profits." It was all so much humbug. Reich must be forgiven because he is in a political job and politics requires people to do strange things, but the public should not be taken in by this sort of headline grabbing. The real issue at the Dayton plant was not safety and health but rather the power of unions to use OSHA in labor disputes.

To be sure, claims of management indifference to safety and health conditions have long been a staple of union efforts to fuel worker distrust and antipathy for management. Whenever a labor dispute is underway, unions routinely flood OSHA with complaints about hazards in the employer's workplace. OSHA inspectors have always been required to sort out such complaints from real ones and in fact have established procedures for doing so.

But union propaganda about unsafe workplaces bears scant relation to the real world. In addition to compelling considerations of human decency, employers have tremendous economic and legal incentives to provide workplaces free of safety and health hazards. Long before OSHA came along, workers' compensation programs and insurance companies were pressuring business to invest more time and resources in identification and elimination of workplace hazards. Since the early 1950s, workplace injuries and illnesses have steadily declined, a trend that was neither interrupted nor accelerated by the activities of OSHA that commenced April 28, 1971.

Then as now, workplace fatalities are the result of bizarre circumstances that are generally not amenable to the enforcement of specific rules and requirements, which is the basis of OSHA action. A full 37 percent of all work-related fatalities are the result of vehicle accidents, and another 16 percent are homicides.

Not long after OSHA became operational in April 1971, I fell into a conversation with some veteran safety inspectors and industrial hygienists discussing the agency's likely impact on their professions. Their assessment was uniformly dismal, even though they knew OSHA would raise the status of their work and bring them enhanced career opportunities. But the underlying principle of OSHA—enforcement of static workplace rules and reliance on legalistic interpretations—struck them as the very antithesis of safety. Safety is a matter of active attention and alert work practices, not blind obedience to arbitrary rules. They predicted the OSHA program would serve mainly to draw resources away from effective programs to reduce injuries and into the hands of lawyers. Some of those old guys are still around, shaking their heads, wondering how long this foolishness will continue.

But OSHA's cockeyed approach to safety is a paragon of rationality compared to its posture on health hazards. It was clear from the outset that OSHA's legalistic style would not offer an effective remedy to health hazards because they are so nebulous and impossible to define.

For example, some scientific studies may suggest that vinyl chloride, benzene, or some other industrial chemical has cancer-causing properties, but there is no way for any physician or scientist to state clearly and unequivocally at what level of exposure such a substance becomes hazardous. Scientists, bureaucrats, and lawyers conduct furious debates regarding various levels of exposure that may or may not be safe—fifty parts per million, fifty parts per billion—like Puritan theologians discussing how many angels can balance on the head of a pin. It is all so much gibberish. None of them has a clue.

But where gibberish is in abundance—Washington, D.C., for example—labor unions perceive fertile ground for troublemaking. From the first days of OSHA, the unions orchestrated a scare campaign about alleged cancer hazards in the workplace. In a speech to the AFL-CIO in 1978, then Secretary of Health, Education and Welfare Joseph Califano alleged that as much as 38 percent of *total* cancers in the United States could be attributed to workplace exposures. Not long afterward, OSHA funded a huge media event in Chicago under the slogan "Is There a Workplace Cancer Epidemic?" in which hundreds of hinterland journalists were wined, dined, and treated to harangues about alleged corporate misdeeds by a variety of social and union activists.

The Califano report has gone down in history as one of the most bizarre abuses of the scientific process since antebellum Southern doctors conjured up an imaginary disease to explain why slaves kept trying to run away from their masters. It was never published in a reputable journal or subjected to the normal peer review. Ten federal researchers were listed as contributors, but seven of them quickly disavowed any connection with it.

Within two years, other researchers had torn it to shreds. In a famous rebuttal published in the *Journal of the National Cancer Institute,* Sir Richard Doll and Richard Peto, two of the world's foremost authorities in cancer epidemiology, offered an exhaustive examination of all cancers in the United States that might be reasonably attributed to external causes—such as smoking, diet, pollution, and occupation. They described the Califano report as "a confidence trick" and said it was probably written "for political rather than scientific purposes."

Yet somehow that spurious report served its purpose in terms of giving labor unions a weapon to wield against business. The truth never quite caught up to it, though responsible journals that had been duped by the original report tried to make amends. "A 1978 study that seemed to represent the views of the government's principal health research agencies concluded that 20 to 38 percent of American cancers are work-related," The *Washington Post* editorialized on August 13, 1981. "Though that conclusion was widely criticized and swiftly repudiated by several of the report's authors, the perception remains that workplace exposures account for a large and growing fraction—some have called it an emerging epidemic—of American cancers." The actual fraction, the *Post* pointed out, was probably more on the order of 2 or 3 percent, but even that was mostly conjecture.

Not long after the Califano report was issued, a group of top corporate leaders in the chemical industry invited a representative of the AFL-CIO to a private meeting to discuss workplace chemical regulation. The corporate brass were weary of protracted legal wrangles about how many molecules of some strange-sounding chemical might or might not present a hazard to workers. They were willing to err on the safe side to protect workers in return for an agreement by the unions to be reasonable. The chemical companies had reason to cut a deal with the unions because they needed to have some idea what level of technological controls they should build into the new chemical plants of the future. The union rep listened politely to the offer and then replied, "Sure, we'll cut a deal with you, just as soon as you stop resisting our organizing efforts in the Southern states."

Thus, the unions perceive OSHA not as an agent of worker safety but as a lever for promoting union power and influence. The preposterous image of the workplace as a hotbed of noxious gases and callous management indifference to worker safety is still gleefully promoted by the unions, and the government continues to issue false reports on health effects in response to union pressures.

Citizens have a right to expect honest and truthful reports from their government. But the Califano report, then the false asbestos scare (that continues), and more recently the bogus report about the effects of secondary cigarette smoke have fairly well established that our government, or at least some key sectors of it, will gladly falsify science in pursuit of political goals. When those goals are being set by labor unions, environmental groups, and consumer activists—watch out! We have squandered vast amounts of our nation's wealth in homage to this abuse of power for which no credible defense can be made.

The small business advocates in the 104th Congress are determined to change the way OSHA does business, and the agency is running scared. Already OSHA has launched a nationwide experiment in which it is focusing its resources primarily on businesses and industries with recognized safety and health problems and offering immunity from penalties to those employers that will cooperate with OSHA and work to eliminate hazards. Not surprisingly, most companies eagerly accept this offer.

This is the sort of enlightened policy OSHA should have adopted years ago. Predictably, the 104th Congress is suspicious of OSHA's motives and determined to rewrite the agency's charter anyway to make certain the changes continue in the future. But any rewrite of OSHA's basic legislation must survive both threat of filibuster in the Senate and veto at the White House. The dilemma of making real changes at OSHA underscores the fragility of the small business revolution to date and the need for continued activism.

WORKERS' COMPENSATION

An interesting sidebar to OSHA's health and safety program is workers' compensation, which, with a few notable exceptions, is run by the states. In many states, liberalized workers' compensation programs have permitted unscrupulous employees to parlay minor ailments into early retirements. Sometimes the afflictions they claim to suffer from have nothing to do with work-related injury or illness but rather are related to drug abuse, alcoholism, sexual conduct, or general psychological stress. The cumulative effect of such abuses is to drive up the cost of workers' compensation for all companies, a burden that falls hardest on small employers.

Indeed, it was the high cost of workers' compensation premiums that drove tens of thousands of businesses to flee California in recent years, greatly adding to that state's economic distress.

However, those who advocate a federal takeover of workers' compensation are barking up the wrong tree. There is absolutely nothing in the federal experience to suggest Uncle Sam would do a better job of sorting out real claims from fake ones than the states do. To the contrary, experience under the infamous black lung program that channels relief checks to former coal miners teaches us that no matter how poorly some states administer workers' compensation, the federal government would do an infinitely worse job of it. The solution for poorly run state workers' compensation programs is for local chambers of commerce to work with their state chamber to secure reasonable reforms from state legislatures.

AFFIRMATIVE ACTION

Of all the regulatory and paperwork hassles that discourage creation of jobs in America, perhaps none is more troublesome than affirmative action. It was originally conceived—like most government programs—as a remedy to a recognized problem. For hundreds of years, women and minorities have been denied equal access to a range of opportunities. President Lyndon Johnson decreed, sensibly I believe, that it was not reasonable to expect them to catch up by themselves overnight. Thus, we embraced affirmative action, enabling disaffected groups to receive priority consideration for opportunities, which presumably helps them to make up lost ground.

But though greater numbers of minorities and women have entered the mainstream workforce in recent years, it is not clear that this is due to affirmative action, stepped-up antidiscrimination enforcement, changing attitudes, or economic factors. However, it is clear that affirmative action—unlike laws against discrimination—provokes widespread resentment. Like the emperor with no clothes, affirmative action requires the public to pretend not to see reality. On the one hand we officially declare as a matter of national policy that discrimination is unacceptable and illegal while on the other hand affirmative action makes it necessary that we not only sanction but actually require discrimination.

Partisans of affirmative action bristle when this is called reverse discrimination, but by whatever name you call it, it is what it is. If I am required by law and other regulatory mandates to give preference to certain individuals because of their gender or race, I am by definition discriminating against others who do not belong to that gender or race. To challenge this interpretation is to deny words their recognized meaning. Defenders of affirmative action resemble the Queen of Hearts in *Through the Looking Glass,* who insists words mean whatever she wants them to mean at a given time.

There is much written these days about angry white males and their presumed rebellion against affirmative action, which was supposedly a major factor in the November 1994 upheaval at the polls. Actually, I don't think there are so many angry white men out there as there are just ordinary people of all races and genders who have grown weary of being forced to pay lip service to what is plainly double-talk—calling discrimination by another name.

According to Shelby Steele, author of *The Content of Our Character,* affirmative action "has always been what might be called iconographic public policy—policy that ostensibly exists to solve a social problem but actually functions as an icon for the self-image people hope to gain by supporting the policy."

But perhaps the most worrisome aspect of affirmative action is that it imparts a stigma to its purported beneficiaries, who quite naturally resent it and wish to be free of it. Shelby Steele and noted economist and commentator Thomas Sowell are by no means the only prominent blacks criticizing affirmative action, and it is not because they believe discrimination is no longer a problem. Rather, they see preferable remedies to racial and gender discrimination that do not provoke resentment or require double-talk and which would not be affected by an end of affirmative action.

It seems hardly a week goes by anymore without yet another report of zany results of affirmative action in action. For example, in Montgomery County, Maryland, where I reside, the local schools are totally committed to affirmative action to the point that the welfare and rights of individual students are often ignored. Recently, in an article published in the *Washington Post,* a white parent related his trials with the county board of education when he was denied permission to transfer his adopted Korean-born teenager to a preferred school because of the potential "impact on diversity." Never mind that the young man in question is no more Asian than Bill Clinton or Bob Dole. His ancestry is all that matters to the board of education. The school he was attending has only eleven "Asian" students, and for that reason the young man was denied permission to transfer into the special French immersion program he wanted to attend. This sort of lunacy goes on every day in the public schools and universities of our nation.

The business community is united in its commitment to equal opportunity. However, there is a split between the larger corporations that long ago made their peace with affirmative action and small businesses that lack the administrative staff to deal with the paperwork or speak the rarified affirmative action language of professional personnel specialists.

The problem small firms face is not simple. High-priced lawyers and judges expend vast amounts of time splitting hairs over which employment practices fall within the ambit of affirmative action and which do not. From time to time, the U.S. Supreme Court revises its position on affirmative action, inevitably rendering the issue even more obtuse. It is no simple thing for any employer to decide among job candidates of comparable qualifications when one of them belongs to a protected group. The most closely reasoned decisions are routinely appealed to higher courts. It is an extremely expensive process that, left unchecked, will go on forever.

An excellent case in point is the notorious *Piscataway* case. In 1989, the Piscataway school district in New Jersey had to dismiss one high school business teacher because of budgetary constraints. The two business teachers with least seniority, Debra Williams and Sharon Taxman, had virtually identical records and credentials. The final decision was to fire Taxman because she is white.

Taxman filed a complaint of discrimination. The U.S. Department of Justice, first under President Bush and then under President Clinton, took her side. The U.S. District Court ruled in Taxman's favor because there was no record of discrimination in that school system or obvious claim for remedial action. The woman had been fired because she was white and that was obviously wrong. End of story.

But wait. The school board appealed the decision. Clinton named a new assistant attorney general for civil rights, Deval Patrick, who persuaded the administration to switch sides. At last report it was before the same court arguing in favor of the obvious discrimination it opposed last year.

The *Piscataway* case underscores how increasingly convoluted the whole affirmative action business has become. The school system had to fire a teacher because it was short of money, but it has since spent many times the amount of a business teacher's salary on this legal dispute, with no end in sight. Most businesses, especially small businesses, cannot afford to squander vast sums of money on such refined legalistic nit-picking.

If all of the top government officials and judges cannot find a clear direction through the affirmative action minefield, it is no wonder that ordinary working people and small business operators are exasperated with it.

I share the opinion expressed by House Speaker Newt Gingrich that we should not simply discard affirmative action without offering an alternative in its place. But we must recognize that the groundwork has shifted dramatically since the 1960s, when affirmative action was first conceptualized, and yesterday's solutions are not appropriate for today's problems. American society is vastly more enlightened and progressive than it was in the 1960s. The overwhelming majority of employers are more than eager to hire and promote minorities and women who can do the job. There is a nationwide commitment to equal opportunity that will never be abandoned, regardless of the fate of affirmative action.

There is one sidebar to affirmative action that truly does drive small businesspeople to distraction: "set-asides" that guarantee a certain percentage of government contracts to minority- and woman-owned firms regardless of their competitiveness, abilities, or track record. In many instances, the companies taking advantage of such set-asides are not true minority firms but employ minorities in conspicuous positions in order to dupe government contracting officers into believing they are minority firms.

THE DAVIS-BACON ACT

Of all the labor law anachronisms that have long since worn out their welcome, few can compare with the Davis-Bacon Act.

Davis-Bacon requires contractors to pay "prevailing wages"

to workers engaged in federally funded construction projects. The Labor Department is responsible for determining exactly what wage levels prevail in different parts of the country at any given time—a most daunting task—for upward of three hundred specific job categories. As a matter of practice, the Labor Department generally deems the local union wage as the "prevailing" one, though it is invariably the highest.

The result of Davis-Bacon is to immunize workers on construction projects funded in whole or in part with federal dollars from competition, thus enabling them to earn much higher wages than they would if the work were subject to normal competitive pressure. As a result it is not uncommon for electricians, carpenters, and other workers employed on federally funded construction projects to earn twice as much as other workers next door doing the same jobs on projects that do not involve federal money. Obviously, this is a great deal for the workers who happen to be doing government work. Equally obviously, it is a terrible deal for those paying for the work, which are the taxpayers. But the most damage is done to aspiring construction workers who do not belong to unions and have not yet mastered the skills that command top wages.

Where Davis-Bacon does not apply, employers are able to hire unskilled laborers and pay them lower wages while they develop their skills. This is the way the free enterprise system is supposed to work—enabling lower income workers to learn on the job, supplementing their skills and improving their economic position. But construction companies cannot afford to pay top dollar, never mind the double rate required by Davis-Bacon, to novices. Ergo, on federally funded construction projects—which involve about one out of four construction jobs in the country—low income workers are being shut out of the market while those already at the top of the scale make out like bandits (or lawyers).

The real-world impact of Davis-Bacon today echoes its sordid origins. Enacted in 1931, the law was deliberately concocted to discourage black laborers from competing for federal construction jobs at a time when those were just about the only construction jobs available. Then as now, Davis-Bacon served to prop up union labor, and when the law was enacted, blacks were routinely denied entry into construction unions.

THE CONTRA COSTA COUNTY CASE

The Davis-Bacon Act not only fosters a great deal of trouble in its own right but also gives rise to similar schemes on the state and local level. For example, only last year the U.S. Chamber of Commerce persuaded the U.S. Court of Appeals for the Ninth Circuit to strike down an ordinance enacted by California's Contra Costa County that required employers to pay "prevailing wages" on private construction projects.

The decision in *U.S. Chamber of Commerce* v. *Bragdon* had implications far beyond Contra Costa County because following adoption of the ordinance on August 21, 1990, several other California counties—including South San Francisco, San Mateo, Belmont, and San Bruno—enacted similar provisions applicable to even smaller contracts. In addition, counties in other states were actively considering such rules.

The ordinance in question was enacted at the behest of union activists trying to recapture construction work that is increasingly being performed by nonunion labor. The idea of requiring construction employers to pay "prevailing wages" was based upon Davis-Bacon. In many instances, the result is to require wage and benefit packages in excess of $30 per hour.

The idea of using the power of county government to require payment of inflated wages by private construction companies was something new on the union scene and struck terror into the hearts of many construction executives. Thus, we resolved to get involved early to nip this terrible idea in the bud.

A few months after adoption of the ordinance, the National Chamber Litigation Center (NCLC) brought suit in the U.S. District Court for the Northern District of California to have it overturned. A public policy law firm affiliated with the U.S. Chamber of Commerce, the NCLC maintained Contra Costa County was preempted by federal laws, specifically the National Labor Relations Act and the Employee Retirement Income Security Act, from setting wage rates for the private sector. The NCLC contended also that such an ordinance violated the contract clauses of both the federal and state constitutions. After lengthy appeals, the U.S. Court of Appeals for the Ninth Circuit upheld the lower court's original decision in a decision handed down on August 24, 1995, almost exactly five years after the original ordinance was adopted, thus administering a well-deserved coup de grâce to it.

Because it is in essence an unfunded mandate, repeal of Davis-Bacon would immediately save taxpayers more than $1 billion per year and, perhaps more important, remove from the marketplace one of the most unjust, ill-conceived, and irrational labor laws ever devised by the hand of man. If there was ever a viable reason for Davis-Bacon, it has long since disappeared. The sooner it is consigned to the history books, the better it will be for all of us.

OTHER HORROR STORIES

After Joseph Hindman was fired by GTE Data Services in Tampa, Florida, for bringing a gun to work, he sued to get his job back under the Americans with Disabilities Act (ADA). In Hindman's view, he was the victim of mental illness aggravated by improper medication and thus legally disabled as defined by the law.

When Ouida Sue Parker left her job with the Schering-Plough pharmaceutical company in Tennessee because of severe depression, she received workers' compensation payments, but she also filed a lawsuit seeking relief under ADA.

Lynn Gansar Zatarian, a television anchorwoman in New Orleans, filed suit under ADA after she was fired for demanding extra time off to take fertility treatments.

The good news is that all three of these lawsuits were unsuccessful. The bad news is that the employers had to pay a bundle to defend themselves in court, and the three cases cited here are representative of a virtual avalanche of ADA litigation now unfolding across the nation. Very few of these cases involve plaintiffs afflicted with legitimate disabilities as most of us understand the term.

One need not travel back to the Great Depression to find labor programs that create more problems than they solve. The Americans with Disabilities Act, passed in the early 1990s, is only now beginning to make its presence known.

Without question, the architects of ADA were motivated by the most noble of intentions, and the goals enshrined in the law are universally admired across the political spectrum. Who could object to extending full opportunities to all citizens regardless of their disabilities or enabling them to reap all of the rewards, tangible and intangible, that stem from honest labor? Certainly, if our nation can more fully use the abilities and energy of all citizens, our economy will be more productive and our society more stable.

But as usually happens, the champions for the rights of disabled Americans and the legislators responding to their pleas did not make sufficient distinctions among legitimate competing interests, respect limitations demanded by real-world constraints, or allow for fiscal limitations of enterprises, organizations, and agencies subject to the law's myriad requirements.

In fact, since ADA went into effect in 1992, more than a third of all complaints filed with the Equal Employment Opportunity Commission (EEOC) have involved claims of back pain, emotional problems, and ailments related to alcoholism and other substance abuse. No more than 6 percent of all ADA complaints filed with the EEOC involved people with sight or hearing impairments. Perhaps most important, the vast majority of actions filed under ADA, some 85 percent, involve people who already have jobs. The original purpose of the law was to help disabled people enter the workforce.

An EEOC analysis of some 40,000 complaints filed under ADA through 1994 showed that the biggest single complaint, accounting for 19.5 percent, involved back problems; 11.4 percent involved "emotional/psychiatric impairments" other than mental retardation; and 3.6 percent were by people who said they are impaired by alcoholism or drug addiction and need protection from employers who want to fire them.

Only 12.1 percent of the complaints were from people with spinal cord injuries and other neurological problems—an area of concern that, along with blindness and deafness, received much discussion when the law was being drafted. A separate category, and one for which the real data are not available, is the expense of retrofitting tens of thousands of workplaces and public facilities with wheelchair ramps, elevators, toilet stalls, and other special provisions to accommodate people with a wide variety of handicaps. Together with the soaring cost of litigation, ADA is proving to be a major expense for both public and private enterprises.

"Employers can hardly be sanguine about the law's seemingly endless scope," labor attorney Louis Pechman wrote in the July 30, 1995, *New York Times.* "Falling within its protective sweep are recovered drug addicts, people suffering from panic attacks, depression, or other mental illness, the learning disabled, the mentally retarded, alcoholics, the obese, individuals with facial disfigurements, and persons who are impaired in their ability to procreate. In addition, the law protects those employees who are not actually disabled but are perceived to be so. For the employee who wants to sue, the ADA has, as my wife likes to say, a lid for every pot."

When ordinary people are called upon to make sense of this hash the results can be truly nutty. For example, because alcoholism is considered a disability under the law, you can't ask someone if he is an alcoholic, but you can ask if he drinks alcohol. "These subtleties are beyond the grasp of most lawyers," Pechman wrote, "let alone the small business owner who meets the law's threshold coverage of 15 employees."

I have no doubt that the ADA has given many employers incentive to hire handicapped people—an effect that would not show up in the EEOC data. Still, it is clear ADA has become yet another weapon in the hands of disgruntled employees with personal axes to grind and little inclination to accept personal responsibility for their own condition. It also has become another compelling reason for small business to remain small, thus avoiding the fifteen-employee cutoff at which employers become liable for ADA action. The 104th Congress can do all of us a big favor by rewriting this law to reduce the potential for abuses.

DISCOURAGED EMPLOYERS

Every time the Labor Department issues unemployment statistics, it includes a separate category for "discouraged workers." These are people who for one reason or another have given up looking for work and thus are not counted among the unemployed.

But the real problem is not discouraged workers but discouraged employers, who have been intimidated by excessive and ill-advised government programs that effectively penalize job creation.

I recently read an analysis of the economic situation in Sweden, where welfare statism is much more advanced than here. The Swedish government has always served as an employer of last resort, but is no longer able to do so. There is too little money and too many people need jobs. The government is appealing to business to pick up the slack, but there are few ears to hear. Only now have Swedish authorities discovered a missing segment of their business community—the all-important midsize companies.

Slightly less than half of all Swedish workers are employed by firms with more than five hundred employees, and slightly less than half work for small family-owned firms with fewer than twenty employees.

The middle ground—the vigorous midsize companies that are the mainstay of our economy—are not to be found in Sweden. "What you find here," said Swedish economist Nils Lundgren, "is that Swedish manufacturing is like its forests—there are a few big fir trees but no underbrush."

Nor is there any wonder why. The high taxes and expensive labor costs imposed by the Swedish government killed the incentive for small firms to grow into midsize companies. Small Swedish firms find it much wiser and less hassle to remain small.

It sounds hauntingly like the machine shop I visited, and hundreds of thousands of other small enterprises in this country. There are many businesses out there that could be creating jobs—good jobs—but the government effectively discourages them from doing so. In effect there is a war on labor carried out under the banner of enlightened concern for working people and with devastating impact. We have had time enough to assess the results of this foolishness and recognize that the time has come to finally put a stop to it.

POVERTY AMERICAN
STYLE

*We do not quite forgive a giver. The hand that
feeds us is in some danger of being bitten.*
—RALPH WALDO EMERSON

C ecelia Mercado is a Connecticut mother who relies upon
Aid to Families with Dependent Children (AFDC) to
feed her eight offspring. In an inspiring display of grit and
ambition, two of her children took part-time jobs to raise
money for college. Eventually they accumulated more than
$1,000, the cutoff line for AFDC recipients. But when the
bureaucrats found out about her children's earnings, Mercado
had to repay the $9,342.75 she had received from the govern-
ment during the time her assets exceeded the minimum and
her kids were required to squander quickly their hard-earned
money so their mother could regain eligibility for AFDC.

A variation of the same thing happened to Grace Capetillo
of Milwaukee, who tried to put away money for her daughter

to attend college. According to an account by columnist William Raspberry, Capetillo not only had to repay more than $15,000 to the government, she also was convicted of welfare fraud and placed on probation.

These stories make me angry not because they reflect bureaucratic foolishness but rather because I understand why the bureaucrats had to punish these women for what most of us would consider admirable efforts to improve their situation. The government has a legal obligation to restrict welfare to people who really need it, hence the $1,000 cutoff line. If you have that much money in the bank, presumably you can afford to buy your own food. Obviously the government should not give money to people who already have money.

Perhaps by now that minimum has been increased to reflect inflation. These events first surfaced in 1992. But whether it's $1,000 or $10,000, the basic problem is the same. When Congress creates welfare programs, it must prescribe arbitrary limits for eligibility. The only other possibility would be to empower anonymous bureaucrats to decide who deserves help and who does not. That would give them extraordinary power over the lives of other people on a level simply not acceptable in a democracy. Our legislature cannot do that, and yet, as these examples demonstrate, an arbitrary limit on eligibility serves to discourage people from breaking out of the welfare trap.

Few issues are as vexing as welfare. It is in a real sense the Achilles' heel of the free enterprise system, the nagging question about what happens to people who, for one reason or another, cannot compete successfully in the marketplace.

On the one hand, we do not subscribe to the socialist doctrine that advocates even distribution of wealth regardless of one's contributions to society. That concept is irrational and unworkable because it flies in the face of everything we know about human nature. In the absence of practical economic incentives, humans become dysfunctional.

I once heard a man say that communism was nothing more than a system in which you weren't allowed to fail. When failure is not permitted, either in enterprises or people, there is no way to sort the good from the bad, the productive from the unproductive, or the efficient from the inefficient. Even worse, people have no objective means of assessing their own worth.

Over time, the bad, unproductive, and inefficient accumulate to the point that nothing works. Any Russian citizen can testify to that—as can the victims of communism in Cuba, Vietnam, Hungary, and dozens of other places.

On the other hand, we cannot stand idly by while people starve in the streets. Our basic notion of welfare is that the government should help people out for as long as it takes them to get back on their feet and become self-sufficient, and no longer.

Unfortunately, our federally operated welfare system has become a sociological black hole, consuming money and people in ever greater gulps. There is a growing consensus among Americans of all social and economic backgrounds that our welfare system, far from helping people get back on their feet, encourages them to remain within the welfare web indefinitely and attracts even more people to enter its grim orbit. It fosters third- and fourth-generation welfare dependency. We have to change it.

The bill for this government-engineered catastrophe is large and growing. In 1994, about 5 million families received Aid to Families with Dependent Children at a cost of $26 billion. Individual recipients numbered 14.2 million, including 9 million children. Food Stamps and Medicaid add more to the welfare tab. In fiscal 1994, Medicaid is expected to spend $169 billion providing medical care to 33 million poor people, up 12 percent from the year before. In June 1994, Food Stamp enrollment reached 27.4 million, an all-time high.

Over the past thirty years, we have spent more than $5.3 trillion in the war on poverty, more than we spent on World War II, a key difference being that we won World War II. Between 1984 and 1994, the Food Stamp program costs rose by $13 billion, or 113 percent, while overall consumer prices were rising only 42.6 percent. Some social aid programs have grown even more. For example, according to Citizens for a Sound Economy, the Women, Infants, and Children program soared from $10.4 million at its inception in 1974 to more than $2.1 billion in 1994.

In 1994, overall federal, state, and local outlays averaged $35,757 for every family of four below the poverty line. More than 75 percent of students under the age of eighteen qualify for free school lunches. The implications for society go far beyond mere dollars and cents, however. No country can consign a significant portion of its population to nonproductivity and expect to prosper for long. A recent survey by Citizens for a Sound Economy affirmed that 91 percent of middle income Americans disapprove of the existing system and want it reformed.

Some people have expressed surprise at learning the U.S. Chamber of Commerce is taking such a keen interest in welfare reform. In truth, while the U.S. Chamber has long advocated "welfare-to-work" programs, our members did not demonstrate much interest in the issue until recently. Now every survey of our business members reveals welfare reform has become a top priority, and for good reason. If our commercial interests are to compete successfully against Asia and Western Europe, they must have a steady supply of educated, motivated workers as well as an affluent domestic market for its products and services. Small businesspeople in particular see the growing welfare population as a real and present threat to their future.

THE TRAGEDY OF POOR CHILDREN

Poverty has a disproportionate impact on children. Most adults can fend for themselves one way or another, but kids cannot. They are for much of their young lives dependent upon family for their basic needs. According to the National Commission on Children, at least one out of every four children under the age of six in the United States is living in "poverty." One out of seven children is in a family receiving AFDC.

Those data offer an ominous warning for the future of our country. Children who are obliged to spend their formative years without the basic necessities of life cannot be expected to grow and mature into useful and productive citizens. To be sure, many children whose families fall below the poverty line receive the basic necessities of life—food, shelter, medical care, discipline, and love. Those of us who were born into the Great Depression and lived through World War II know you don't need a fat bank account and two late-model cars to have a solid family and get a good start in life.

I personally was born into a poor family and know well the rigors and hardship that accompany genuine need. At the same time, we all know children from affluent families who are starved for moral and ethical guidance. There is a lot more to this issue than money.

Amid the great wealth that characterizes the United States in the 1990s, we have developed a rather lofty concept of poverty. "To the typical citizen, saying someone is 'poor' implies he lacks a decent place to live, is short on food or clothing, or perhaps that he needs a car to get to work and doesn't have one," wrote Robert Rector in *American Enterprise* magazine. "By this commonsense standard, very few of the 39 million 'poor persons' identified by the Census Bureau are, in fact, poor. In 1993, nearly 40 percent of all 'poor' households owned their own homes. Nearly 60 percent of 'poor' households have more than two rooms per person. Nearly 60 percent have air-conditioning. Sixty-four percent of 'poor' households own a car; 14 percent own two or more cars."

It goes without saying that hundreds of millions of people in this beleaguered world would give their eye teeth to share in such "poverty," which from their point of view could easily be mistaken for affluence.

Some years ago a group of American leftists went on a "sharing" tour in the Soviet Union to establish their solidarity with the communist revolution. They took along a film version of Steinbeck's *The Grapes of Wrath* with its stark depiction of displaced Oklahomans caught up in the Great Depression. Their purpose was to affirm Soviet propaganda about the evils of capitalism. But the gesture backfired. The Soviet citizens were unimpressed by the "poverty" of Steinbeck's Okies, which seemed ordinary by their standards.

But what did impress them was the ability of the Okies to go climb in their truck and strike out for greener pastures in California. Within the Soviet scheme of things, the power of an individual family to just get up, get into a vehicle of their own, and drive anywhere in the country they wanted to go was an awe-inspiring display of wealth and freedom.

"I will never forget the American film made from Steinbeck's [*The*] *Grapes of Wrath*," wrote Lev Navrozov in his 1975 work *The Education of Lev Navrozov*. "The author and the filmmakers wanted to show the life of the poor in the thirties. The poor rode about in trucks. The Russian audience stared. Even a small dingy car thirty years old is a status symbol here, perhaps as high as a yacht in the United States. But the ownership of a truck is something as would, in the United States, be the ownership of, say, a fleet of dirigibles. The audience perceived Steinbeck's wrathful message of poverty as a futuristic fantasy about extraterrestrials riding about in their fleets of dirigibles."

The wealth of the United States forces us to a new and more sophisticated definition of poverty. Unlike in many other nations, the "poor" of America do not generally go hungry or cold or sleep in the street, unless by choice. There are soup kitchens and overnight shelters available to most anyone who will observe minimal rules of decency, respect for others, and abstinence from alcohol and illegal drugs. Even medical care is available on demand at most public hospitals to indigent people with no money. To starve to death in America in this day and age one must really work at it.

Occasionally we read of street people freezing to death, but they are almost always mentally unhinged or substance abusers who refuse offers of assistance. American cities, despite their problems of crime and poverty, have not yet descended to third world status.

Within the context of our society, poverty refers to people who for one reason or another cannot pay their own way and are dependent upon government aid for basic support—food, housing, and medical care. Each year their numbers increase while expensive programs designed to get them off welfare produce minimal results. Most troubling of all, a disturbing number of welfare recipients appear to be raising a large number of children in a manner that virtually guarantees that they also will become wards of the state. The American people are increasingly frustrated by this stubborn social pattern and determined to change it.

TOUGH LOVE

In 1987, the then and future mayor of Washington, Marion Barry, was touring a homeless shelter when he encountered a

welfare recipient named Jacqueline Williams who had fourteen children. "Why don't you find me a better place to live?"
Williams demanded. "Why don't you stop having all those babies?" Barry replied.

Barry lived to regret that candid comment—he had to go
on *Donahue* and explain himself—but it was a priceless moment of candor from a public official not noted for it. Mayor
Barry spoke for a lot of us that day, and his question remains
unanswered. For as long as people like Jacqueline Williams
continue to produce illegitimate children without a clue how
to provide for them, our welfare dilemma will continue to get
worse.

There is a presumption among most observers that a new
approach to welfare reform is coming and it will have a
tougher edge than former efforts. There is much talk of limiting welfare to certain time frames and, perhaps most signifi-
cantly, cutting off assistance to welfare mothers who continue
to have illegitimate children. "For too long we have defined
compassion according to the number of people who are on
AFDC, food stamps, and public housing," says freshman Republican Congressman J. C. Watts of Oklahoma. "I suggest
we should define compassion according to how *few* people are
on AFDC, food stamps, and public housing."

We must begin with candid recognition that poverty American style is largely a product of foolish individual lifestyle decisions. Foremost among these is an increasingly common
willingness of ill-educated poor people to have children out of
wedlock. Indeed, it is fair to say that while not all poverty
stems from this cause, the epidemic of poverty we see breaking
out nationwide is almost exclusively a byproduct of fatherless
homes.

In 1960, 2 percent of white births and 22 percent of black
births were illegitimate. By 1991, the white rate of illegitimacy

was up to 22 percent and the black rate had soared to 68 percent.

About 40 percent of welfare mothers have their first child while in their teens, and about half of all teen mothers go on AFDC within four years of giving birth. The "deadbeat dads," meanwhile, are nowhere to be found. Those are frightening data that convey a dismal picture of children having children long before they are mature enough to understand fully the implications of parenthood.

We cannot make a blanket assertion that two parents are always better than one because there are always cases in which the offenses of one parent are so grave and destructive that family breakup is imperative. Nevertheless, all of the data at hand confirm what we know instinctively and from experience, to wit: a caring two-parent family is infinitely more likely to do a decent job of raising kids than a similar one-parent family.

All of us who have raised children know how demanding and exhausting it can be. Merely earning enough money to keep a family housed, fed, and clothed is a major challenge for most people. In the modern era, most families must send both parents into the workforce to make ends meet. That of necessity leaves both parents scrambling to get kids to school, get dinner cooked, clean the house, and perform all the myriad tasks associated with family life. With one parent absent, something has to give, most likely the time allotted to discipline and guidance.

"Compared with teenagers of similar background who grow up with both parents at home," report sociologists Sara McLanahan and Gary Sandefur, "adolescents who have lived apart from one parent are twice as likely to drop out of high school, twice as likely to have a child before age twenty, and one and a half times as likely" to be out of school and in the workforce in their early twenties.

Single parenthood is "damaging to children in so many ways

that to list them individually would be to trivialize them," writes social scientist Charles Murray, who concludes that "illegitimacy is the single most important social problem of our time . . . because it drives everything else."

Obviously, any effective remedy to this most vexing challenge must include serious incentives and disincentives for both the mothers and fathers of illegitimate children. While we threaten to withhold financial aid to women who continue to have illegitimate children, we must at the same time get deadly serious about tracking down "deadbeat dads" and making them provide for their offspring. Requiring this investment will give absent fathers incentive to take a more active personal interest in their children as well.

The Crime Epidemic

Much anxiety about welfare stems from its clear connection to the crime epidemic that is transforming major parts of our great cities into combat zones. Young men without positive role models at home, especially young men whose mothers are themselves young and poorly educated, all too easily become menaces to society. Even the more jaded among our police and prosecutors profess themselves baffled by the current crop of young hoodlums who seem to lack any sense of right and wrong. They are often compared to savage predators in the jungle, except that predators are predictable and usually kill for a reason—to satisfy their hunger. It has become an almost daily occurrence in America's major cities to read of horrendous crimes committed by youths on momentary whim without provocation, purpose, or sense of shame. There is something bloodcurdling about what is going on that speaks to a fundamental disruption of the social fabric.

More than 70 percent of all juveniles in state reform institutions come from fatherless homes. "The relationship between crime and one-parent families is so powerful that controlling for family structure erases the relationship between crime and race and between crime and low income," asserts Jennifer E. Marshall of the Family Research Council. "The role of the traditional two-parent family is essential in sustaining the institutions of a free society precisely because it is the vehicle by which values are transmitted from generation to generation. If the family fails to impart values that temper and restrain behavior, broad legal freedoms must give way."

Every time this subject comes up, we get another round of public education bashing. To be sure, there is much within the educational establishment that cries out for reform. But the schools were created to teach academics, not moral character. There is an old African saying that it takes an entire village to raise a child.

Edmund Burke, the eighteenth-century British philosopher and statesman, offered profound insights on how a society promotes and reinforces civilized behavior. The first germ of affection in a person, he said, is to be attached to the subdivision, the "little platoon," that one belongs to. Through daily contact, interaction, and sharing with those immediately around us, we learn positive life habits and draw strength from others also engaged in that learning process. The little platoon, Burke said, is the first link in the series by which we proceed toward a love of our country and of all mankind.

The schools are a critical link in the chain, but only one. The young people running wild on the streets of America lack useful workplace skills, but the problem runs much deeper than that. Amitai Etzioni, director of George Washington University's Center for Policy Research, refers to a "psychic underdevelopment" that characterizes all too many of these children of the underclass. The unemployables, he believes, are kids who in their high school years have not been helped by their families to develop such attitudes as industriousness, respect for rules and authority, and self-discipline. When schools lack a strong code of discipline and rigorous academic demands, they make the problem worse instead of better. "As a result, many young people are unable, for psychic reasons, first to learn effectively in the schools, and then to function effectively in the adult world of work, community, and citizenship. Thus, the root problem is not that millions of high school graduates have great difficulties in reading, writing, and 'rithmetic; these all-too-common deficiencies are consequences of insufficient self-discipline, of inadequate ability to mobilize self and to commit."

Stated in plain English, these kids lack the kind of discipline most of our parents gave us—insistence that we do our homework, clean our rooms, perform our chores, meet our commitments. That is how we learn to put business before pleasure, to do the work before we take time to play, and to do the honest thing when it is not convenient to. We learn by example and from application of external pressure—constant, direct, and unremitting—to control our most destructive impulses, to think before we act, and to respect laws and authority. That is how young people learn to be good citizens and productive workers. The government cannot do that for kids; only families can.

But the families caught up in the welfare trap are increasingly unable to do it. Two scholars at the Brookings Institution, John DiIulio of Princeton and Donald Kettl of the University of Wisconsin, point out that barely 1 percent of adults receiving welfare work for their benefits. "As a group, long-term female AFDC recipients are second only to male and female long-term prisoners in terms of the number and severity of life problems they carry: learning disabilities, substance abuse problems, physical abuse and neglect as children or adults, teen pregnancies, and more."

According to *U.S. News & World Report,* currently 25 to

40 percent of long-term AFDC recipients have handicaps that prevent them from holding full-time jobs. Two-thirds of those who have been on the AFDC rolls for more than two years have not graduated from high school, and the average adult on welfare has eighth-grade reading and math skills.

These people are unable to impart positive life values to their children because they have none to impart. The communities they live in cannot offer the missing guidance because it isn't to be found. The respectable residents have long since fled to the suburbs to escape the inner city pathologies. In sum, many of these kids are growing up in a moral and ethical vacuum.

This is not a uniquely American dilemma or an unprecedented situation. As long ago as 1744, the lord mayor and aldermen of London drew up an address to the king in which they stated that various "confederacies of great numbers of ill-disposed persons, armed with bludgeons, pistols, cutlasses and other dangerous weapons, infest not only the private lanes and passages, but likewise the public streets and places of usual concourse, and commit the most dangerous outrages upon the persons of your majesty's subjects." Eight years later the writer Horace Walpole reported that "One is forced to travel even at noon as if one were going to battle."

Today, London is one of the safest major cities in the world and violent crimes are exceedingly rare. We can address our crime problem effectively by recognizing it as a component of the welfare challenge and dealing with it on that basis.

ROLLING UP OUR SLEEVES

In December 1994, the General Accounting Office reported that only 11 percent of the 4.6 million parents on AFDC participate monthly in any of the education, training, or job search programs set up by the 1988 Family Support Act. Social workers trying to prod AFDC recipients into real jobs are amazed to discover they must coach the applicants to say "good-bye" and "thank you" when they leave job interviews. Roughly a third of those who live on public assistance cannot read a street map or fill out a Social Security card application. Many are afflicted by alcoholism, drug addiction, and depression.

In many other cases, according to *U.S. News & World Report,* the problem is simple lack of aptitude. "Most AFDC recipients score too low on intelligence tests to qualify for the armed forces, and nearly half of young AFDC mothers score below the eighteenth percentile for all women."

Notwithstanding all of these dismal facts and statistics, we can help many of these people rise above their mean condition and assume productive places in the workforce. A few years ago, the Tulsa Chamber of Commerce in Tulsa, Oklahoma, was approached by one of its members, Zebco, Inc., which is a major supplier to Wal-Mart. Wal-Mart prefers to sell products made in the United States, but at the time it was unable to find a domestic maker of fishing rods. The challenge was to find domestic workers who would help the supplier set up an assembly line for fishing rods.

The Tulsa Chamber created a nonprofit corporation known as the Industrial Exchange (IndEx) to provide AFDC recipients with employment experience and remedial education. IndEx provides welfare recipients with four hours of actual job experience in the morning and four hours of custom education in the afternoon. All eight hours of manufacturing and education are conducted in one building with on-site day care available.

A major component of the program was cooperation from government to reduce the paperwork and relax regulatory requirements that always hinder such innovative experiments. The Oklahoma Department of Health and Human Services case workers refer clients to IndEx. Clients sign contracts to become participants and agree to adhere to a rigorous schedule.

Zebco, Inc., has since been joined by three other industrial firms that supply IndEx with work projects to train participants in manufacturing skills. Academic and specific skill training is provided through the Tulsa Public Schools, the Tulsa Technology Center, Tulsa Junior College, and the University Center at Tulsa.

Several aspects of this demonstration project warrant a hard look. For starters, it was begun by a real industrial opportunity that was not being filled and now is. The state government was willing to bend the rules where necessary to stop penalizing employers for creating jobs. There was and remains a continuing cooperation among business, the local chamber of commerce, state agencies, public schools, and universities to work with AFDC mothers to help them make the transition from welfare to work. Most important, the welfare mothers were not suddenly thrown into a job on their own without support or means of taking care of their children. IndEx is predicated on the assumption that many AFDC recipients lack the basic workplace ethic and skills that we tend to take for granted. Everywhere they turn, people in the IndEx program find support, encouragement, and cooperation.

Since the program was created, roughly two hundred welfare recipients have participated in IndEx. More than seventy have been placed permanently in private sector manufacturing jobs earning $9 to $10 per hour. That is an astounding success rate.

The experience in Tulsa—and other places—shows it can be done and also how to do it. Business, government, and academia must work together and provide each participant with one-on-one contact and support. If we are to interrupt the welfare cycle, we must provide aid recipients with the moral and ethical guidance they have never received to help them then pass that guidance along to their own children.

DRAWING A LINE

Most of the debate about welfare reform lies across that basic fault line between the free enterprise and collective philosophies of government. We resent giving people money to sustain laziness and vice, but we are reluctant to see people go without the basic necessities of life.

The proposal drawing the most fire would enforce arbitrary limits on how long a person could draw AFDC. Polls show a majority of Americans support such limits, but tough-minded views often become shaky when confronted by hard reality. After the Battle of Waterloo, when it was suggested that Napoleon should be executed, the Duke of Wellington said, "If the emperor is to be put to death, someone should be appointed as his executioner, and that someone should not be me."

I have a strong suspicion this debate will continue for a long time, regardless of what Congress does to our welfare system, because when it comes time to cut poor people off relief there will be fierce resistance from those who must do the dirty work. Like the Iron Duke, they will suggest someone else be given the assignment.

Returning responsibility and money to the states to handle welfare-to-work programs is the best way to begin. To be sure, there will be a great variety of programs among the states, and some will work better than others. But I am confident none will do worse than what we are doing now. As the experience in Tulsa has demonstrated, when people closest to the problem become actively involved and have authority to bend the rules, real progress is possible.

There must be a presumption by all parties that welfare is a transition leading to work, not a permanent condition. To make that happen, business must be involved all along the way. There are many basic jobs, such as making fishing rods, that are not being done because there is no one to do them. Welfare recipients have no work to do. Innovative minds on the local level can come up with countless ideas like that. Such creativity simply does not exist in Washington, and if it did, it could not surmount the federal bureaucracy. That fact alone is reason enough to return authority to the local level.

Every welfare recipient must be immediately put on a job track, and if that means further education and training is necessary, it should begin at once. The longer it waits, the longer the recipient has to become addicted to welfare. The education and training must be conducted by public or private education and training providers in coordination with local businesses and in response to the skills needed by local business. Many local chambers of commerce are already taking a lead role in this process. More will become involved if given the opportunity to experiment free of regulatory restraints and bureaucratic interference.

Similarly, social workers already in the welfare bureaucracy must receive priority training to be effective in a new environment in which rigid rules are pushed aside in favor of active engagement with real people and ad hoc problem solving.

Part of the education mix must include basic stuff about work that most of us take for granted, such as the importance of being at work on time, how to dress, how to interact with customers and coworkers, and how to follow instructions.

It is absolutely imperative that all of this be conducted in a drug-free environment and that everyone involved be informed of this requirement in no uncertain terms from the outset. Similarly, drug-free status must be a basic of eligibility for federal welfare benefits. This is one hard-and-fast rule that even Wellington would agree to enforce. Drug abuse is the scourge of modern society and no segment of our population is more vulnerable to its wicked embrace than the poor. Anyone who applies to participate in the new "welfare transition" must agree to abstain from drugs and to submit to periodic testing for drug use—without qualifications.

Finally, we need a holiday from federal regulations for businesses that agree to participate in the "welfare transition" program. Because almost every applicant and employee can select from a long list of possible reasons to sue an employer, business has huge disincentives to hire even well-qualified welfare recipients.

Many Americans, most not receiving welfare, have embraced the victim mentality and are eager to attribute responsibility for their problems and failures to someone else. Every adverse employment decision is a pretext for litigation. In some jurisdictions, it is virtually impossible to discharge an employee for any reason. Asking employers to hire welfare recipients raises all kinds of red flags because they are people who have become accustomed to receiving something for nothing. Part of welfare transition reform must be a holiday, perhaps six months, from liability under federal laws that provide for lawsuits and other actions against employers by employees. The social activists will howl and the lawyers will protest, but that is the best criterion I know of for determining the value of an initiative.

A BRUSH WITH REALITY

In the autumn of 1995, the left-wing magazine *The Nation* assaulted cutbacks in welfare spending as "the liberal Gettysburg, the turning point in the defense of American social democracy," and said it represented a "bipartisan agreement that the United States bears no responsibility for its poorest families." Continuing in that same vein, *The Nation* said Democrats had joined in the Republican assault on welfare "because of a widespread perception that the welfare system breeds dependency," a view that stems from "a concerted right-wing ideological campaign and party from changing attitudes toward women and work."

"I'd say it stems mostly from an unpleasant decades-long brush with reality," opined commentator William Raspberry in response to *The Nation* article. "The way we have dealt with poverty—though it has eased the plight of many of the least-damaged poor—really has bred dependency. The severing of the connection between exertion and income—however generous the impulse or meager the income—can do long-term harm—yes, including the increase in births to unwed teenagers that the conservatives keep shrieking about."

Raspberry zeroed in on the fundamental problem in the welfare debate—which is the same in the debates about the environment, workplace conditions, consumer product safety, and legal reforms—the excessively partisan tone of the debate that makes rational discussion almost impossible. "As a result we have a sort of pretend debate between the 'mean-spirited right' and the 'naive and soft-headed left'—caricatures that mask our shared dilemma."

Raspberry contends we have to lay the political rhetoric and ideological warfare aside and work together to find practical ways to wean welfare recipients away from their dependency. I couldn't agree more. In the short term, it will probably cost more than it does now to help people get off welfare, but if that is the price we must pay to end welfare dependency, let's get on with it.

"Nothing ever comes to one that is worth having," wrote Booker T. Washington, "except as a result of hard work." Most people, even those in the most deprived circumstances, will seize an opportunity to become self-sufficient if they can see it clearly in front of them and have incentive to take it. The threat of losing benefits, as cruel as it may sound, will in many cases be the decisive incentive they need. Likewise, harsh measures to discourage illegitimacy will also have effect. In sum, we must combine the carrot—real opportunities to learn job skills and access to jobs that offer a clear and believable path to lifetime learning and earning—with the stick—reduction or elimination of benefits. It is a hard thing to do, but leaving people in the existing situation is far more cruel.

7

Spotted Owls Are Red Herrings

*When the oak is felled the whole forest echoes
its fall, but a hundred acorns are sown in silence
by an unnoticed breeze.*
—THOMAS CARLYLE

In the autumn of 1993, several residents of southern California, fearful of potential brush fires that frequently ravage the area, applied for permission to plow firebreaks around their homes. Their application was denied by the U.S. Fish and Wildlife Service because bureaucrats feared the firebreaks might encroach upon the habitat of an endangered species of rat. "In three minutes my house was consumed in flames," said homeowner Anna Klimko after the fires swept through her neighborhood, "and in seven minutes everything was gone. For what? A rat?"

Ah yes, but this is no ordinary rat we're talking about but rather the now-famous Tipton kangaroo rat, so called because of its somewhat elongated rear legs, which bear a faint resemblance to the unrelated marsupials of Australia. In nearby Riverside County, Cindy and Andy Domenigoni were forced to idle eight hundred acres of fertile cropland, losing several thousand dollars in annual income, to preserve habitat for the same rat species.

On February 20, 1994, a phalanx of some two dozen government agents invaded the farm of Taung Ming-Lin, an immigrant from Taiwan, and charged him with killing a Tipton kangaroo rat. Lin had immigrated to the United States in 1991 and bought 719 acres from Tenneco Oil Company about one hundred miles north of Los Angeles. Lin wanted to raise vegetables and was assured by Kern County officials the land was suitable for that purpose, but he was threatened with one year in prison and potential fines of $300,000 for violating the Endangered Species Act. Welcome to the land of freedom and opportunity, Lin!

Brandt Child planned to build a campground and golf course on his property near Moab, Utah, which is noted for its scenic beauty and proximity to two national parks. But the project came to an abrupt halt when the U.S. Fish and Wildlife Service decided the natural springs on Child's property were a habitat for the endangered Kanab Amber snail. Ah yes, the famous Kanab Amber snail, storied in fact and fiction. Child's land was subsequently fenced off by the government and he has been forbidden to do anything significant with it. Predictably, the property is now deemed worthless by the real estate market. Child calculated his loss at $2.5 million.

Meanwhile, an alleged threat to the Furbish lousewort was employed to derail a dam construction in Maine, and the beleaguered condition of the ever popular Oregon silverspot butterfly was used to thwart plans for a $100 million resort on the Oregon coast.

One of the more interesting aspects of the government's solicitude for endangered species is that surviving members of the species do not need to be scarce to be deemed endangered. There are, for example, an estimated 15,000 to 17,000 golden-cheeked warblers flying around Texas eating insects, laying eggs, and doing all the customary bird stuff. But in 1990, the U.S. Fish and Wildlife Service declared the tiny fowl endangered, and in 1994 the agency proposed to declare some 800,000 acres in thirty-three Texas counties to be critical habitat. A goodly portion of this land is valuable property near Austin, the capital of Texas.

This advocacy of the golden-cheeked warbler endangers the economic status of many people. For example, Howard Burris of Travis County was ordered to cease a development project on his land, which his family has owned since World War II. Before the warbler was listed as endangered, his land had been valued at $1.5 million, but land that cannot be used has no value. The bank foreclosed on his four hundred acres.

"I'm not at all opposed to protecting endangered species," said Burris, "just to giving up my net worth to do it."

An endangered species does not have to be few in number nor does it have to actually be present in the "critical habitat." Near San Francisco, the Shorelands Company bought 740 acres of barren clay flats. After the company spent $12 million on a development project, the U.S. Fish and Wildlife Service declared the site to be a potential habitat for the endangered California clapper rail, the California least tern, and the salt marsh harvest mouse. Not one of those species currently lives in the area, but that is beside the point. You just never know when one of those clapper rails or harvest mice might decide to drop in and visit a spell. The Shorelands Company was forced to file for bankruptcy.

In Washington state, the U.S. Fish and Wildlife Service is seeking to prevent the Anderson & Middleton Logging Company from harvesting timber on 72 acres of privately owned land in order to protect a pair of spotted owls nesting a mile and a half away on government land. Again, you just never know when they might want to drop by.

Perhaps no other species has caused quite as much fuss as the spotted owl, a rather innocuous bird known for no particular achievement other than a hotly disputed flirtation with extinction and which, for some reason, is presumed by the government to live only in old-growth forests. The great spotted owl contretemps began with a 1986 report from the Audubon Society claiming that the birds had dwindled to fifteen hundred mating pairs—which some experts claim is the critical cutoff line denoting imminent extinction. Subsequently, a government panel decided Uncle Sam should endeavor to ensure survival of at least three thousand pairs. In 1991, federal judge William Dwyer banned most logging in Washington and Oregon to save those three thousand spotted owls.

In 1994, the Clinton administration issued its own spotted owl plan which, in effect, will impose the judge's restraining order on the Northwest forever. The impact on the region's economy is profound. The administration's plan will prohibit harvesting of roughly four billion board feet of timber, mostly Douglas fir. At the 1991 price of $395 per thousand board feet, the plan is permanently locking up $1.6 billion in raw timber. Since the 1991 ban went into effect, the cost of lumber has shot up enough to add $5,000 to the cost of an average home.

Somewhere between 9,500 jobs (the Clinton administration's estimate) and 85,000 jobs (the timber industry's estimate) are being destroyed. The people being hit hardest by this are not the yuppie professional weekend backpackers whose avowed love of nature gave birth to the logging ban and who work in air-conditioned offices and can easily absorb an extra $5,000 on the price of a house. Rather, it is the blue-collar working people who sweat for their pay, struggle to send their kids to college, and are the first to be laid off when clumsily written environmental laws are misused by extremists to impede economic development.

I use the term "misused" carefully, for the fate of the spotted owl was never a matter of great concern to the environmentalists seeking the logging ban. Subsequent investigations by scientists, some employed by logging companies and others by the environmental groups themselves, confirm there are many more spotted owls around than previously thought.

The entire owl controversy was predicated on assumptions that spotted owls live only in old-growth forests and that the species in question is restricted to Washington and Oregon. But we now know that six to eight thousand pairs of spotted owls live in northern California—where the government once claimed there were none—in timberland that is managed and regularly harvested.

The latter fact is pivotal, for it appears that spotted owls do quite well outside old-growth forest, thank you very much, and for a perfectly rational reason. The floors of old-growth forests tend to be fairly sterile because overhead canopies of leaves prevent light from reaching the ground. But the ample sunlight and dense undergrowth that characterize new forests create a superb habitat for the small mammals that owls feed on.

According to environmental writer Gregg Easterbrook, as many as ten thousand pairs of spotted owls may live in the western states. As David Wilcove, a biodiversity expert for the Environmental Defense Fund, says, "It appears that the spotted owl population is not in as bad a shape as imagined ten years ago, or even five years ago."

But the discovery of more owls and correction of earlier false reports of the owls' scarcity has had absolutely no impact on the continuing logging ban in the Northwest or the economic havoc and personal tragedies that ensued in its wake. The environmentalists who first brought the lawsuits leading to the ban do not care one whit that the entire episode is predicated upon a falsehood, nor do the federal agencies involved, nor does the Clinton administration, nor does the federal judiciary. Owls or no owls, the logging ban remains.

One would think the federal judge who issued the order, confronted with this subsequent information, might want to revisit the issue, lift the ban, and admit it was all a mistake. But the law doesn't work that way. Once the process has begun, it assumes a life of its own.

Not even the quest for scientific knowledge is immune from the ravages of extremists in the environmental movement. A case in point is the observatory on Mount Graham, Arizona, established by a group of world-reknowned astronomers.

Environmentalists used alleged threats to the Mount Graham red squirrel to stop construction. The astronomers determined it would take an act of Congress to overcome opposition to the project, and an act of Congress was duly obtained, but even with that the environmentalists have been able to use the Endangered Species Act to deter completion of what would be the world's most powerful binocular optical-infrared telescope.

For all that, there is substantial evidence that the Mount Graham red squirrel is not a distinct species at all but rather just another one of the twenty-four subpopulations of red squirrels common throughout the Southwest. "The only way we can know for sure that it's a Mount Graham red squirrel," says University of Arizona biologist Bruce Walsh, "is that it was taken on Mount Graham."

ORIGIN OF THE ENDANGERED SPECIES SCAM

The use of phony endangered species claims to forestall a variety of development projects, which has since become a regular scam orchestrated by extremist environmental groups, began back in 1973 when a biologist from the University of

Tennessee discovered an unusual fish living in a small spring feeding into the Little Tennessee River. He called it the snail darter because he had seen it eating small snails. This was four months before the Endangered Species Act became law.

As it happened the Tennessee Valley Authority was in the process of building the Tellico Dam on the Little Tennessee River against the wishes of local environmental groups, who would soon file a petition with the U.S. Fish and Wildlife Service to put the snail darter on the endangered species list. This was done on October 9, 1975. The following May the U.S. Fish and Wildlife Service declared the Little Tennessee River to be a critical habitat for the snail darter, and in January 1977 the Sixth Circuit Court of Appeals halted the dam project.

On June 15, 1978, the Supreme Court ruled 6 to 3 in *TVA v. Hill* that, no matter how senseless and irrational it might seem, the Endangered Species Act prohibited completion of the dam. The decision, wrote Chief Justice Warren E. Burger, "may seem curious to some" but the law "admits of no exceptions." Congress, Burger continued, made it "abundantly clear that the balance had been struck in favor of endangered species."

Congress, of course, never intended to suspend $50 million dams to prolong the dubious existence of obscure fish. It voted almost immediately to exempt the Tellico Dam from the Endangered Species Act.

Unfortunately, the same outrage and indignation that saved the Tellico Dam did not coalesce into a serious review of the law itself. The Endangered Species Act remains and most of those who run afoul of its arbitrary restrictions do not carry the weight of a $50 million project or the political muscle of the Tennessee Valley Authority. When the victim is an individual or a small business and the issue only a few million dollars, Congress does not intervene. The outrages committed in the name of the Endangered Species Act continue unabated.

A report issued by Citizens for a Sound Economy in November 1994 cited 853 species already on the endangered list and another 3,900 candidates for the list. Most are obscure creatures such as the Hay's Spring amphipod, the dusky seaside sparrow, the Mount Graham red squirrel, and the never overrated Bruneau hotsprings snail. In many cases, it is not at all clear that the species in question is a species distinct from other close relatives. For example, learned ornithologists disagree as to whether the California spotted owl and the northern spotted owl are different species or whether they differ in any significant way from the Mexican spotted owl. Either way, there are more than enough owls to go around.

In addition, there is mounting evidence that the U.S. Fish and Wildlife Service's endangered species program is, like most bureaucratic programs, managed poorly. Some twenty-four species have been removed from the endangered list. Eight were officially determined to have been mistakenly identified in the first place, and another eight were removed on the premise that they had recovered.

However, in five of those eight cases, it wasn't a matter of recovery but rather discovery of additional populations that weren't known about when the original listing was made. Meanwhile, six species became extinct after being listed, and thirty-four others became extinct while on the waiting list.

In truth, the U.S. Fish and Wildlife Service has actual data on populations of only about 20 percent of the species among the 853 on the endangered list. Stated another way, a full 80 percent of the species officially classified as endangered may not be.

But none of that really matters to the extremists who promote this lunacy because the spotted owl—like the snail darter and kangaroo rat—is a red herring, a convenient pretext to throw a monkey wrench into the gearbox of vital development projects in the name of preventing mankind from having its way with Mother Nature.

Without question, there are some stands of old-growth forest that should be preserved for their aesthetic and biologic properties, some of which are not yet fully understood. Like Old Faithful or the Grand Canyon, they comprise some of our greatest scenic wonders and it is imperative they be kept inviolate for posterity.

But propaganda that all old-growth forests are being hacked down willy-nilly is nonsense. There are over 7.5 million acres of virgin old-growth forests on federal lands in Oregon and Washington, and more than 4.2 million of those acres were already off limits to harvest before this controversy began. Harvest is the correct term—not destruction, despoliation, rape, or any of the other pejorative terms routinely invoked by environmental groups. Trees are a renewable resource that when managed properly can sustain our needs indefinitely. Annual timber growth exceeds harvest by 37 percent, or 30.4 billion board feet, and yearly growth in the federally owned National Forest System exceeds harvest by 55 percent.

As for the issue of endangered species, exclusive of its use as a pretext to block development, that issue also cries out for a reality check. Environmental activists have done an impressive job of convincing the public that millions of plant and animal species are being driven rapidly to extinction. When this "catastrophe" is not invoked to block timber harvest in the Northwest, it is used to block timber harvest in the tropical rain forests, mainly in Central and South America.

This issue is legitimate. Wide swaths of biologically sensitive territory, much of it in equatorial regions, are under tremendous stress and many species of plant and animal life are being eradicated. In the process, many irrecoverable secrets of nature are being lost forever. We humans are part of a complex ecological chain and cannot expect to remain indifferent to major disruptions of natural continuity.

But we must keep in mind that millions of species arose and disappeared long before mankind came on the scene. We know about them from fossil records. To suggest that the disappearance of any one species—or hundreds of species for that matter—heralds a catastrophe, as many environmentalists do, is an exercise in inflated rhetoric, not cogent thought. The fabled dodo bird of Reunion Island is gone forever, as is the moa of New Zealand. We all mourn their passing, but life goes on without them. Humankind may one day join the ghostly parade of defunct species, but the jury on that is still out.

Much of the data on disappearing species is based upon studies of species that have disappeared from islands. However, such data should not be applied to large land masses. If a species exists on only one island and dies out, it is gone for good. But a species under stress on a large land mass has a variety of options and more often than not will survive by moving somewhere else.

Likewise, much of the data on disappearing rain forests is exaggerated. Up to half of the tropical rain forests cut down or burned are transformed not into wasteland but into secondary forest. These secondary plants and forests support ecosystems different from those of the primary forest, and they may support less diversity, but they are not total ecological losses.

Perhaps the most conspicuous flaw in reports of ecological apocalypse is lack of information. Those who prophesy the destruction of millions of species have no idea how many species there actually are today or how many existed a million years before humans came along.

Nature has proven time and again her remarkable resiliency. The world abounds in verdant forest tracts that were years ago laid waste by man or natural calamity. Countless species of plants and animals flourish amid soaring trees where once there were only stumps and weeds. There is an extraordinary life force at work on this timeless orb that atones for many of our mistakes. In any event, the needs of humans warrant full and equal treatment to those of owls and snail darters.

PROTECTING WETLANDS

Endangered species offer one pretext for blocking development; protecting wetlands offers another. Only a few years ago, wetlands were widely regarded as a public nuisance and a health hazard. Any effort to drain and fill them was deemed an improvement. There is something about a swamp that seems to demand human intervention.

We now know that the watery slime so offensive to human sensibilities serves as an incubator for a variety of wildlife. Wetlands are not only recognized as a fertile habitat for many species but also as a geologic structure that recharges and purifies groundwater while inhibiting flooding and erosion. The national goal of "no net loss of wetlands," established by the Bush administration, enjoys broad public support.

Unfortunately, there is no problem so vexing that government cannot make it worse or that unprincipled extremists will not misuse for ulterior motives. The federal approach to protecting wetlands is a veritable Frankenstein of laws and regulations that has evolved into a major threat to the basic property rights that underpin our social and economic life. Uncle Sam has defined wetlands as any land saturated for 5 percent or more of the growing season and has hydric soils and hydrophilic vegetation such as cattails and milkweed. Many tracts that appear dry as the Sahara are legally wetlands—which occasions frequent government proscriptions against seemingly innocent human activities and provokes outrage from citizens who do not appreciate the triumph of bureaucratic legalism over rationality.

The issue is not small. There are about 100 million acres of wetlands in the lower forty-eight states. They are mostly on private land and are strategically located where people want to build homes and businesses, roads and pipelines, farms and mines. Indeed, there seems to be an unnatural attraction between wetlands and development similar to that between trailer parks and tornados.

In any case, development of a wetland is illegal except for the smallest parcels, without a Section 404 permit from the Army Corps of Engineers, and all wetlands are considered equal, regardless of size or relative utility to birds and plants.

Although the regulatory standard requires evaluation of a permit application within sixty days, the Corps fails to meet this deadline more than 90 percent of the time. On average, the Corps takes well over a year to process a permit, according to a study conducted by Beveridge and Diamond, a law firm in Washington, D.C. This has been true for wetlands less than half the size of a Ping-Pong table.

To further complicate matters, the EPA can step in and veto any such permit request at any point in the process and impose further delays, replete with legal and administrative paperwork and costs. Landowners who get caught up in this bureaucratic runaround receive no compensation for their economic loss as a result of wetland determination. The bureaucrats, as always, are indifferent to the economic consequences of their actions, as are the environmental extremists who promote and defend this program.

"The general rule, at least, is that while property may be regulated to a certain extent, if regulation goes too far, it will be recognized as a taking," wrote Supreme Court Justice Oliver Wendell Holmes Jr. The wetlands program may have wandered across the hazy dividing line between reasonable stewardship of natural resources and unconstitutional "takings" of private property.

ENERGY DEPENDENCY

While environmentalists have a knee-jerk reaction against routine development, such as the construction of houses and factories and the harvesting of timber, they seem to reserve a special animus for development of energy supplies.

More than twenty years after the first oil embargo threw the economy of the United States into a tailspin, our country remains even more vulnerable to another such disruption in large measure because of unwise government policies promoted by environmental extremism.

We would do well to ponder the anguish of those turbulent years. The oil embargo of 1973 was followed by another in 1978. Consumers waited impatiently in long lines to get gas. Oil prices soared from $3 per barrel to $35 per barrel. Inflation tripled and unemployment doubled. It was a major economic crisis with serious social and political repercussions.

Yet today we are setting ourselves up for an even bigger fall. Oil imports in 1995 account for much more than half of domestic consumption, up from 27 percent in 1985. The Department of Energy predicts we will rely on foreign supplies for 60 percent of our oil by the year 2010.

To some extent, all of this is the inevitable result of declining productivity of U.S. oil fields and the discovery of large reserves overseas. If other nations provide a steady supply of petroleum at less cost than we can, it makes economic sense to take advantage of it. Just as rising oil prices stoked inflation in the 1970s, low oil prices have helped keep inflation under control in the 1990s.

At the same time, it is dangerous for us to become overly dependent upon foreign nations for oil, especially when many of the major oil producers are noted for their political instability and even more especially when there is no need for it. We have extensive oil reserves on the Outer Continental Shelf that we can develop with minimal difficulty, and a potentially huge reserve in the Alaskan National Wildlife Refuge (ANWR) on the North Slope of Alaska. That we have denied ourselves these reasonable options is compelling evidence of the malignancy of environmental extremism in this country and its apparent stranglehold on public policy. There was no significant environmental harm associated with the development of oil reserves at Prudhoe Bay, and there is simply no reason to fear that any sort of environmental catastrophe would accompany development of oil reserves on the North Slope of Alaska. Indeed, we have every reason to develop oil reserves on the North Slope because the Prudhoe Bay field is rapidly declining and will soon leave the pipeline to the lower forty-eight without enough volume to justify its use.

As for the Outer Continental Shelf (OCS), the Interior Department estimates it could contain more than 31 trillion cubic feet of gas and 30 billion barrels of recoverable oil. There is even less danger of environmental damage from OCS development than from the ANWR. But environmental groups, driven by abiding hatred of any kind of development and empowered by a compliant news media and sympathetic government agencies, have so distorted reality that Congress has placed both the ANWR and the OCS virtually out of reach of development. The probusiness faction of the 104th Congress seems more inclined to permit balanced development of these valuable resources, but so far it has been stymied by resistance in the Senate and, as always, a threatened veto by President Clinton.

LANDFILLS AHOY!

Of all the frauds that have been perpetrated in the name of environmentalism in recent years—and there are many contenders for the title—none can compete in terms of wholesale public brainwashing with the mania for curbside recycling of household garbage.

This dubious movement dates back to the *Mobro,* the famous unwanted garbage barge that spent several highly publicized weeks plying the Eastern coastline looking for a place to dump refuse from Islip on Long Island. The gist of the story, as told by our ever imaginative news media, was that the nation's garbage dumps were filled to overflowing and there was nowhere for that New York offal to go.

The true story of the *Mobro,* as documented by the *Wall Street Journal,* was less cosmic but more sinister. It was supposed to be the initial voyage of what would become a regular transfer of New York trash to other places organized and controlled by the Lucchese family, a branch of the Mafia. Unfortunately, the people trying to launch the enterprise were inexperienced and had not nailed down a deal with an established landfill to accept the trash before the *Mobro* went to sea. When the *Mobro* began showing up at various sites, unannounced and uninvited, it provoked concerns among managers of potential sites that it might contain hazardous wastes of some kind. Still later, as the news media began its perverse mistelling of the saga, other dump sites determined they did not want to become known as a receptacle for New York's trash. Two months later, the *Mobro* returned to New York and its load was burned in a Brooklyn incinerator. The most maddening thing about the *Mobro* saga is that the one issue trumpeted over and over by the news media was never an issue: there was not then nor is there now any realistic shortage of landfill space for human garbage. Because, in part, the private sector has established "mega-landfills" that serve large populations.

Always eager to be in the forefront of mythmaking, the EPA subsequently warned in 1988 of a "deluge of garbage." J. Winston Porter, who was then assistant EPA administrator for solid waste, called upon municipalities to create recycling plans that would reduce disposal needs by 25 percent. "We're running out of space to bury it," he wrote in a report, *The Solid Waste Dilemma.*

As usually happens with environmental issues, reality was simply ignored or suspended. Before long, the mythical shortage of landfill space was permanently etched on the American mind and remains so to this day. All across the nation, tens of millions of citizens dutifully do their part every week, sorting out their garbage according to its content and leaving it to be picked up by different garbage collectors.

A closer look at that EPA report, however, raises many questions. A subsequent study said average dumps had 21.3 years of remaining capacity that could be easily expanded with a little effort. "I've always wondered where that crap about a landfill-capacity crisis came from," Allen Geswein, an EPA solid waste official and one of the authors of the study, told the *Wall Street Journal.*

J. Winston Porter has likewise disavowed that 1988 report in favor of a more balanced, economically sound approach to recycling. "The nation has more than doubled the recycling of its trash in just the last six years," he wrote in a commentary published in the *Sacramento Bee* on March 4, 1995. "But there is a downside. Some states, notably California, have set costly and unreachable recycling mandates that may not be obtainable at any price."

It is all a fantasy with simply no basis in reality or rational justification, economic or environmental. The United States is a vast country with literally hundreds of square miles of land, unwanted and unused. Current landfill sites are more than sufficient to handle all of the trash expected to be generated for the next several years. When existing landfill space is used up, there are abundant tracts available for new ones.

The landfill hoax might not matter except that recycling programs are costing taxpayers a bundle and some are polluting the atmosphere in the bargain. Recycling makes good economic sense for industry, where huge volumes of material are involved. It almost always lowers raw materials costs in manufacturing, reduces energy consumption, and in some cases reduces air and water pollution produced by the manufacturing process. Entrepreneurs are working overtime to come up with creative uses for recycled industrial materials, and the markets for such material remain strong. But the logistics of picking up tiny increments of garbage for recycling make it a losing proposition economically.

For example, while San Jose, California, was slashing its budget for libraries and parks to save money, it was losing $5 million a year on its curbside recycling program (which it eventually shut down). Minnesota gives a $7 per month rebate to each household that sorts its trash, even though every additional recycler drives up its costs. New York City, with all of its financial woes, is now facing a $100 million additional expense required by a court order that it obey its own law mandating that 25 percent of all trash be recycled.

"In virtually every community, adding a curbside recycling program increases costs," says Barbara J. Stevens, president of Ecodata, Inc., a Connecticut consulting firm. "City councilmen are shocked to find this out. But it's like moving from once-a-week garbage collection to twice a week."

All of those extra trash pickups mean more trucks on the road pumping more emissions into the air. The city of Los Angeles, with its notorious air pollution problems, now has a fleet of eight hundred garbage trucks on the streets handling all of the various categories of trash. If all of the trash were lumped together, said a city sanitation official, they could pick it up with four hundred trucks.

Like so many regulatory initiatives, recycling is a ritual acted out not because of its beneficial impact on the environment but because it enables people to feel better about themselves. It is another triumph of good intentions over reality.

CONSERVATION VERSUS PROTECTIONISM

The excesses committed in the name of ecology are partly attributable to a major schism in the movement that makes it difficult to sort out fact from fiction. Conservationism and protectionism, the two competing strains of the movement, have been at loggerheads for the better part of this century. The early leaders of the conservation movement, most notably President Theodore Roosevelt and his chief of forestry, Gifford Pinchot, advocated rational development of natural resources. They espoused a concept called "highest use," which meant forfeiting the near-term benefits of immediate development in favor of long-term development.

The preservationists, on the other hand, are philosophical heirs to an influential nature buff from California named John Muir who advocated preservation of wilderness in its natural state, completely free of any human development other than minimal access to enable people to visit but not remain.

Both conservationists and preservationists advocate perpetual protection of wilderness areas noted for their scenic beauty, remarkable topographical formations, and potential for recreational activities. But the preservationists aspire to ban all human development of substantial tracts of land that offer no conspicuous qualities other than a presumed high level of ecological life. Basically, it comes down to forbidding humans access to a substantial portion of the natural landscape for no other reason than a presumption that human activity is bad.

This concept of preserving natural resources has provoked an ongoing series of battles between preservationists and a variety of interests—timber operations, farmers, mining companies. One might think that the business interests would have more sway, but the results suggest otherwise. In 1979, for example, preservationists pressured Congress into setting aside 750,000 acres in Idaho as the Sawtooth Wilderness and National Recreational Area. A resource survey, not completed until after Sawtooth was set up, showed that the area contained an estimated billion dollars' worth of molybdenum, zinc, silver, and gold. According to an article in *Harper's* magazine by William Tucker, "The same tract also contained a potential source of cobalt, an important mineral for which we are now dependent on foreign sources for 97 percent of what we use."

But then, from what we see of their indifference to other economic interests associated with natural resources such as timber and oil, there is no reason to suspect the preservationists would have been moved by revelation of the vast assets lying beneath Sawtooth. Their attitude is one of undisguised contempt for the human factor in nature, with special aversion to the exploitative adventures of capitalists in search of profit.

This romantic attachment to nature is not a recent invention and can be traced back at least as far as the eighteenth-century French philosopher Jean Jacques Rousseau, who wrote rapturously of the glories of nature and the primitive superiority of the "noble savage." This mentality was a forerunner of modern urbanites who savor fantasies of bucolic life on the farm before the age of machines and advanced technology allegedly reduced us to cogs in a great industrial machine. Their mistake is to imagine life on the farm at 5 P.M. instead of 5 A.M., when it actually begins. Our ancestors, whose lives were all too often squandered amid the groaning monotony of endless farm chores and the backbreaking manual labor they demanded, would have given anything to trade places with us. They would have seen our cars, air-conditioned offices, plush carpets, and myriad electric appliances not as distractions from primal life values but as liberators. That we would actually aspire to return to primitive agricultural life would surely strike them as quite insane.

The fascination of modern preservationists with the natural wilderness is likewise a bizarre distortion of the human thought process, a triumph of imagination over reality. The preservationists dream of a simple life that never existed and aspire to communion with nature that invariably seems more inviting from a distance than it does close up. When one is actually out in the wilderness, as I often am, the first and most persistent impression is of the absence of basic tools of living and of all the various complications that come into play when one wishes to perform the most essential of tasks—such as fixing a meal or preparing a secure place to sleep—without the accoutrements of modern civilization.

If people want to indulge in fantasies about the glories of nature, that is their business. If people aspire to preserve certain remarkable tracts of pristine wilderness for posterity's enjoyment, that deserves serious consideration. But those who would deliberately place off limits to human development vast tracts of land for no other reason than a presumption that humanity is an evil force amid a virtuous natural order of things have taken leave of their senses and should not be accorded credence in public debate. The greatest force of nature—the most awesome manifestation of natural power—is the human mind. Where preservationism is in the ascendancy of public discourse, that natural power is at low ebb.

The legislation pertaining to protection of wetlands and endangered species is clearly being abused by extremists pursuing ulterior motives. The laws must be amended to discourage such abuses and also to tighten up definitions of wetlands and endangered species to make certain they are not applied haphazardly, as is now the case. If not, all sense of purpose and balance will be lost.

8

WHY GOVERNMENT IS
THE PROBLEM

*If the state could effectively govern the details of
our lives, no tyranny would have ever been
overthrown.* —GEORGE STIGLER

I n 1980, when schools in the District of Columbia enrolled
150,000 students, the superintendent of schools drove
himself to work and got along with three aides, including
one lawyer. By 1995, when school enrollment had dwindled to
around 60,000, the superintendent was riding to work in a
chauffeur-driven car and ably supported by nine lawyers, a
speech writer, two executive assistants, one special assistant, a
legislative counsel, one administrative assistant, a communications director, and an assistant press secretary. In addition, he
could call upon the support of one vice superintendent, two
deputy superintendents, and a group of associate superintendents, assistant superintendents, and directors, each of whom
commands a personal retinue of his or her own.

Meanwhile, the D.C. Board of Education, which is among the highest paid in the country, was advertising for an executive secretary to be paid $65,000 to $82,000. That salary is not out of line for an organization that counts among its rank-and-file employees 220 who make $65,000 to $82,000 and seven more earning up to $85,000.

This overpaid bureaucratic bloat was made public only because the District of Columbia is bankrupt and demanding vast infusions of fresh cash from Congress. According to Mayor Marion Barry, there is no fat to be cut from the D.C. budget. Meanwhile, the superintendent of schools is asking private citizens to donate free labor to make needed repairs in the public schools because, he said, there is no money in the budget for it. He did not acknowledge any connection between his top-heavy bureaucracy and the shortage of maintenance funds.

Across town the Federal Energy Regulatory Commission (FERC) is still steamed because a few years ago a federal court made it accept money it didn't want. (An editorial I wrote about this incident was reprinted in *Reader's Digest,* to FERC's great annoyance.) FERC is an independent agency that sets rates for sale of electricity and for transportation of oil and natural gas. It is forever hosting long-winded hearings about what rates should be, and there is usually much demand for transcripts of these hearings, which can sell for as much as $6 per page.

Not surprisingly, when the contract to transcribe the hearings came up for renewal, several firms offered to do it for nothing, knowing they could make a handsome profit selling the transcripts to interested parties. But the company that had been doing the work, Ace-Federal Reporters, made the best offer—to pay FERC $7,900 per year for the privilege.

But FERC would have none of it and canceled the solicitation, awarding the contract to one of the firms that offered to work for free. Ace-Federal then upped its offer to $1 million for a five-year contract, but FERC wasn't having any. So Ace-Federal went to court and a federal judge finally ordered FERC to give Ace-Federal the contract at its original offer of $7,900 per year.

These anecdotes about government, one local and one federal, speak volumes about the upside-down mentality that prevails in bureaucracy, why the Soviet Union's bureaucracy eventually strangled that once mighty nation, and why our own country remains in danger not from external threat but from the internal dangers of creeping bureaucracy.

The people who run the D.C. schools simply cannot see any direct relationship between their legions of paper pushers with inflated salaries and the decline of D.C. schools, nor can they recognize their pivotal role in the fiscal catastrophe that has descended upon the District. The people who run FERC saw no interconnection among themselves, the federal budget deficit, and the $1 million Ace-Federal wanted to pay them. That money would have gone to the federal treasury, not FERC, so it was really of no interest to FERC bureaucrats.

Federal bureaucrats are conditioned to move money out the door as quickly as possible, not take it in, because of the budget process that defines their status. If they have funds left over at the end of the year, Congress may decide they are getting too much money and reduce their budget appropriation. From their point of view, it is in their interest to be broke at the end of the fiscal year—and they generally are, which is a major reason the federal budget is always in the red.

When you take away the normal economic incentives that govern the human experience, the result is increasingly bizarre and destructive behavior. Among the normal economic incentives missing from the bureaucracy is that which governs relationships between employers and employees in the private sector. Generally speaking, employees in the private sector who work hard and are productive are rewarded and promoted. Those who are indifferent to their job and rude to the boss get passed over. Those who repeatedly screw up and are conspicuously incompetent get the sack.

But not in the bureaucracy, where firing is almost unheard of and almost everyone gets promoted at the same pace, regardless of their productivity or lack of it. The resulting mentality is something that must be seen to be believed, and it actually can be seen—from a distance. In any normal office of professional workers, of which there are many in Washington, the men and women are well dressed and clearly in sync with the world around them. They observe normal proprieties and endeavor to be efficient and courteous to each other and the public. The competitive pressures they are subject to offer incentive for them to work hard and observe high standards of performance and personal comportment. Their supervisors are constantly giving them feedback on how to improve their standing, which they eagerly accept and respond to.

By contrast, bureaucrats tend to regard advice from superiors as an affront and are not shy about saying so. There is no penalty for being impertinent to supervisors who, in turn, quickly learn to keep their advice to themselves.

Often employees who have grievances toward superiors and animus toward coworkers simply cut off communications and refuse to have anything more to do with them. Such breakdowns in communication would be intolerable in a for-profit organization but are commonplace in the bureaucracy, where no one has authority to force subordinates to work together.

As for relations with the public, rudeness seems almost a prerequisite of government employment. From time to time, federal managers attempt to set up central telephone lines so the public can obtain timely information about agency activities and get answers to complex questions. But in order to maintain such a system, the manager would have to have the authority to hire and retain conscientious employees, and no federal manager, either political appointee or civil service, has such authority. Within a few days, people who call the number hear taped invitations to leave messages, which are never answered. After a brief interval, the number is disconnected and everything is as it was before.

GOVERNMENT EXCESS

Just about every new administration that comes to Washington recognizes the obvious ineptitude of the federal bureaucracy and offers a grand plan to rectify the situation. President Clinton was no exception and his National Performance Review, managed by Vice President Gore, has managed to eliminate tens of thousands of bureaucratic jobs in a relatively short period of time.

But despite the cost savings associated with reducing the government workforce, cutting the payroll does not address the inherent bureaucratic culture that rewards mediocrity, strangles initiative, and denies responsibility. This culture is largely culpable for the frequent bureaucratic excesses that stir so much indignation in the small business community and also present the major impediment to meaningful reform.

Philip K. Howard, author of *The Death of Common Sense,* contends that the answer to regulatory overkill by federal bureaucrats is to authorize government employees to exercise independent judgment and to then hold them accountable for their decisions. "The detail of regulatory law would stun most people—and it's not there for any constructive purpose but to try to keep out any human judgment. The problem is, the stuff gets so complicated that no one understands it. And the rule-books are so dense that no one actually reads them."

In Howard's view, OSHA's hundreds of pages of rules for machinery should be replaced with one sentence stating:

"Tools and equipment should be reasonably suited for the use intended, in accordance with industry standards." Thereafter, OSHA inspectors would make independent decisions as to whether machinery was appropriate. In other words, Howard proposes to infuse the public sector with private sector values.

But Howard recognizes the built-in inefficiencies of the bureaucracy that mitigate against any such experiment in flexibility. "Now, there are also legitimate concerns about the quality of our civil service. You have to have good people doing these jobs, and you have to keep folks on their toes. In some ways, and for some people, government has turned into a kind of public dole. In order to have a system in which you give people discretion and allow them to use their judgment, you need to be able to hold people accountable for bad decisions. Today, you can barely fire people who don't come to work.

"It's amazing to me," he continues, "that public employee unions defend bad performers, as if the people who pay the price aren't their coworkers. It's incredibly dispiriting to work with slackards. And when there are bad civil servants, they cast all government programs into disrepute. That's how most citizens see government—through the people they have contact with."

CORRUPT LANGUAGE

It is not surprising that within the corrupt culture of bureaucracy a unique language has evolved, the purpose of which is to make simple thoughts sound profound and the absence of thought sound sublime. Veteran bureaucrats construct long-winded paragraphs full of subjects, verbs, and all of the other customary parts of speech that grace the English language yet have no meaning whatsoever.

For example, bureaucrats never use something—they utilize it; they never talk to each other—they interface; and no bureaucrat worth his step increase will ever do his best—he will rather optimize his programmatic input in order to maximize productivity parameters personnelwise.

The gibberish of which I speak is well known in Washington and frequently the butt of jokes devised by the bureaucrats themselves who understand full well the vacuum of thought and dearth of action that lies behind their inflated rhetoric. One such is the following chart, which can be used to devise typical bureaucratic phrases that sound impressive but mean nothing. Select any three-digit number at random and use it to compose your own bureaucratese:

A	B	C
1. Integrated	1. Management	1. Options
2. Total	2. Organizational	2. Flexibility
3. Systematized	3. Monitored	3. Capability
4. Parallel	4. Reciprocal	4. Mobility
5. Functional	5. Digital	5. Programming
6. Responsive	6. Logistical	6. Concept
7. Optimal	7. Transitional	7. Time-phase
8. Synchronized	8. Incremental	8. Projection
9. Compatible	9. Third generation	9. Hardware
10. Balanced	10. Policy	10. Contingency

Thus, a simple number such as 587 gives you a "functional incremental time-phase"; a 319 gives you "systematized management hardware"; and 623 produces "responsive organizational capability." Who could be against that? Certainly not me.

During my time with the National Aeronautics and Space Administration, when we were putting men on the moon for the first time, I was quite impressed by the quality of people working for the government. But those were different times at an unusual agency pursuing a visionary mission. It is worth noting that just about all of NASA's work on the rocket program was farmed out to private contractors. It is worth noting also that many top NASA officials had been recruited from outside government and were exempted from civil service regulations, including restrictions on pay levels.

To be sure, there are in every bureaucracy individuals who take their jobs seriously and perform prodigiously despite the absence of practical incentives. But take any one of those individuals off to the side out of earshot of their colleagues and inquire if they do not know of employees who contribute nothing but trouble to the agency they work for, who continue to receive regular pay increases despite lackluster performance, who regularly defy supervisors and perform below par, and who haven't the faintest notion of giving a fair day's work for a fair day's pay. I guarantee you any honest bureaucrat will roll his or her eyes and tell you of dozens of such people—and assure you also that they could get a lot more work done if such deadwood were pruned from the staff and not replaced.

An executive of a private corporation can give instructions and reasonably expect that they will be carried out, for he or she has the power to discipline anyone who does not meet their responsibility, and also to reward superior performance. A chief executive can recognize and nourish talent throughout the ranks on an ad hoc basis, subject only to normal employment procedures and legal requirements.

No such power exists in the public sector. "Out of 120,000 people in the Treasury, I was able to select 25, maybe," notes former Treasury Secretary Michael Blumenthal, who served during the Carter administration. "The other 119,975 are outside my control." Blumenthal has referred to federal bureaucracy as an "inverted pyramid" where people at the top, generally political employees or members of the senior executive service, do most of the work and cannot delegate. "There are, of course, others at lower levels who are equally dedicated, but what I'm saying is that the rank-and-file, because of the way the system is organized, tend to be less efficient and slower and more bureaucratic. I'm not saying they couldn't be led. If we had the possibility to lead them, if we had the possibility to motivate them, if we had the possibility to hire and fire them, to move them around, they would function as well as anyone else. There's nothing inherent in a bureaucrat that makes him less efficient. It's the way the system is structured. So I'm not indicting the people; I'm indicting the system. It's an important distinction."

And yet it is undeniable that the system is so perverse that it does terrible things to the way people caught up in it think and operate, as evidenced by the behavior of the D.C. school officials, FERC, or any other federal, state, or local government agency you care to name.

Some years ago, Meg Greenfield, editorial page editor of the *Washington Post,* recalled an encounter with the bureaucratic mentality that made a lasting impression on her and other members of *Post* management:

I once worked in an office with a woman who had come to us directly from a long and successful stint in the federal government. I don't say that she was representative of all her kind, only that she ably represented one strain of it: *she saw to it that nothing ever got completely done.* This was her gift, and as I came to understand it, after some initial eruptions of temper, what she had been expected to do in her previous job and what she therefore thought would make us happy. Every project she was asked by us to undertake, even the simplest yes-or-no, what-was-the-date-of kind, stretched on toward infinity, unimaginatively hobbled by complications and detours on which she would periodically report back to us—this was 'getting done,' that could probably be resolved when the library clips on the subject were returned next week by X, who had the flu, but whose wife said he hoped to return to work on Thursday, depending on whether the doctor would see him Tuesday. But of course this was still chancy, because the doctor was out of town, etc. It was finally terminally maddening, and the woman is no longer part of our enterprise. But her message was very important, and she lingers on with me. She explains a lot about Washington in general and our poky political metabolism in particular.

That is not to say that there are not rude and incompetent employees in the private sector, only that there are natural forces at work to weed them out, and sooner or later they do get weeded out. But not in the bureaucracy, save by death or retirement. The bureaucratic work environment is a disaster for the people caught up in it and for the country that relies upon the bureaucracy for vital services. It is a disaster that gets progressively worse with each passing year.

A LOST CAUSE

The bureaucracy, with its built-in incompetence, unmanageability, and lack of accountability, bears much of the responsibility for the regulatory horror stories that abound and the growing public resistance to higher taxes and bigger government.

It is simple enough for Congress to mandate safer workplaces and a cleaner environment and all of its other highblown regulatory objectives, but after Congress has done its work and gone home, it is the bureaucracy that is entrusted to enforce Congress's will. The results—when there are results—are often bizarre.

More often than not the loudest critics are people who actually work in the bureaucracy. Like the major-city schoolteachers who send their own kids to private school, the bureaucrats are first in line to demand limits to bureaucratic power and influence.

A survey of 1,003 Americans conducted on behalf of the nonpartisan Council for Excellence in Government by pollsters Peter Hart and Robert Teeter, released in April 1995, concluded that three out of four Americans believe government "could be effective" if it had a better workforce. (Incidentally, Hart is a Democratic poll taker and Teeter is affiliated with the Republicans, so the survey truly was bipartisan.) "When people look at the federal government trying to deliver services, they see example after example of inefficiency," Teeter said. "If you talk to business executives, they say decentralize, push decision making down, and hold people accountable."

When apportioning blame for the failures of government, the survey showed that Americans focused on people instead of programs. The federal government's greatest weakness, 61 percent said, was wasting money "because it is not well managed," and 56 percent said it "spends too much money on the wrong things."

Hart noted "a certain contempt that people have for federal workers" because "when they have an interaction . . . it's usually not a favorable experience."

Dismay with the federal bureaucracy was the major factor leading 64 percent of respondents to support a shift of authority from the federal level to the states. "The idea of pushing back programs to the states is very strong," Teeter said. "But it shouldn't surprise us. In business, when decision making is pushed down, quality improves. People see this all the time in their daily lives."

This is why the very notion of federal bureaucrats being entrusted with the nation's health care system was enough to make our blood run cold and why small business reacted so violently to the Clinton health care reform plan.

The nation got a preview of what Clinton care would look like in 1993 when Congress, at Clinton's behest, enacted the Vaccines for Children program. This was a classic example of big government advocates misunderstanding a problem and designing a government solution guaranteed to make it worse.

The problem was and remains that many children under the age of two do not receive proper vaccinations. The Clinton administration assumed this could only be due to price gouging by pharmaceutical companies and thus designed a federally supported program to rectify what they perceived to be a clear-cut case of corporate indifference to public need.

Somewhere along the line, it was pointed out that most parents paid to have their kids vaccinated, and the Vaccines for Children program would simply subsidize the middle class at government expense to do what it was already doing.

So President Clinton agreed to a more limited program by which the government would buy one-third of the nation's vaccine supply and set up a distribution system to provide it to the needy.

There were two problems with this grand scheme. First, the main reason many kids don't get vaccinated has nothing to do with corporate greed but rather with the ignorance or lack of attention of their parents. As Senator Nancy Kassebaum, Republican from Kansas, warned at the time, "Too many parents do not know the value of vaccinations."

Oddly, however, though barely half of the nation's two-year-olds are vaccinated, almost all of the five-year-olds are. The reason seems to be that they have to be vaccinated to get into kindergarten. When parents encounter this obstacle, they finally get off the dime and have their kids vaccinated. But to President Clinton it is clearly an issue of evil drug manufacturers pursuing "profits at the expense of our children."

The second problem with the Clinton scheme, and the truly fatal one, was its reliance upon the federal bureaucracy to buy up all that vaccine and get it to the kids. It is simply amazing that after all these years and all the bureaucratic snafus that are common knowledge, anyone still thinks Uncle Sam's troops can handle something that complicated.

The General Accounting Office was called in to review the situation, and anyone could have predicted what the GAO discovered. The government was way behind in setting up the purchase contracts, unprepared to evaluate if the system could effectively process orders, and unprepared to test whether its storage and delivery system would preserve the integrity of the vaccines, which are vulnerable to changes in temperature. In short, the Clintonites were just assuming the federal bureaucracy could and would administer their complex project efficiently and effectively just like, well, a private corporation.

Now the Vaccines for Children program has become a new bureaucratic monster with a life of its own. It began modestly two years ago and is already consuming $843 million of your tax dollars a year with no end in sight.

"To say, after describing a social economic problem, that the state must do something about it," wrote Nobel Prize–winning economist George Stigler, in a memorable essay, "is equivalent in rationality to calling for a dance to placate an angry spirit. In fact, the advantage is with the Indians, who were sure to get some useful exercise. The state can do many things, and must do certain absolutely fundamental things, but it is not an Aladdin's lamp."

AN ANCIENT DILEMMA

The fundamental issue before us as a nation is to reassess the proper relationship between the public and private sectors, with a decided emphasis on returning more autonomy to both individuals and private enterprises. In an ideal world, the public sector can be expected to serve as a court of last resort to rectify inequity and injustice but not as an Aladdin's lamp for transforming the human experience into a postindustrial utopia. The driving power in human events lies in individuals pursuing their dreams and ambitions and the private sector enterprises they forge in the process. The government is there, like a referee at a ball game, to make sure the players observe the rules in an atmosphere of open and honest competition. When the referees begin calling the plays and deciding who gets in the game, the entire system begins to bog down. Our guiding purpose should be to encourage efficient government and restrict it to a minimal agenda that does not strain its capacity nor excite unrealistic expectations among the citizens.

The campaign to pare back Uncle Sam's bloated ranks and curb his appetite for power and influence is long overdue. But we cannot eliminate all government responsibilities or abandon its all-important role as society's referee. Hand in hand with the belt-tightening must come a new concept of government management. We need a concerted effort to address the cultural currents endemic to the bureaucratic culture that mitigate against efficiency, productivity, and common sense. No group of people is better suited by temperament, experience, and judgment for this task than the small business contingent driving the political revolution.

9

A Vision for the Millennium

❖

Where there is no vision, the people perish.
—ISAIAH

Fifty years ago, the American military brought down the curtain on the deadliest conflict in human history, in which an estimated 45 million people perished. World War II was a pivotal cataclysm that propelled us from the ranks of secondary world powers into the forefront of world leadership. We had not bargained on that result, but nations rarely anticipate the consequences of war. As writer-historian William Manchester sagely observed, most soldiers fight for the one thing they cannot possible have—restoration of the status quo that prevailed before the war began. War forges a reality of its own that always takes the participants by surprise.

Certainly the Germans and Japanese did not anticipate the catastrophic conclusion of their great adventures in militarism nor that humiliating defeat would set the stage for their resurgence a generation later as even greater powers based upon economic rather than military prowess.

Our elevation to world dominance was disconcerting to many Americans mainly because we came so far so quickly. Throughout the 1930s we had been embroiled in a vicious economic implosion known to history as the Great Depression. In a time when there was no social safety net, a fourth of all workers were unemployed. Even that horrendous statistic understates the severity of the crisis, for almost every one of those unemployed workers was sole breadwinner for a family with few other resources. Despite a decade of government efforts to get the economy going again, the unemployment rate was still 17 percent in 1939.

It is telling that one out of four young men drafted for military service was rejected as physically unfit largely because of the effects of insufficient diet during the Great Depression. We who can recall those difficult days are at a loss to explain what it was like to the current generation born to affluence and opportunity. They do not understand that there was a time, not so long ago, when hard-working middle-class Americans sent their children to bed hungry.

The war brought a sudden end to the Great Depression. Almost overnight we went from double-digit unemployment to virtually full employment. Everyone who was not eligible for military service was needed in war production. Workers who had never dealt with heavy machinery or electricity were thrown into incredibly disorganized construction projects roaring full tilt twenty-four hours a day, lit up by klieg lights during the night. Safety was not a priority. The workplace carnage that ensued rivaled that of many battlefields, but few protested. The entire world was engulfed in a titanic struggle between starkly drawn forces of good and evil. The nation's survival was clearly at stake. Citizens rolled up their sleeves and went to work. There was a remarkable unanimity of spirit and commitment that many today remember with fondness, despite the many hardships we endured.

Our industrial base proved decisive in the conflict. Had the Germans and Japanese appreciated our ability to flood the allied arsenal with war materiel, they might have thought twice about their aggression. When Hitler was informed late in the war of the true scope of American production, he dismissed the report as unbelievable. His skepticism was understandable. In the four years the United States was in the war, our industries produced 296,351 aircraft of various types, 102,351 combat tanks and self-propelled guns, 372,431 artillery pieces, 87,620 warships, 2,716 Liberty cargo ships, and 44 billion rounds of ammunition.

The truly remarkable thing is that this production was achieved from an industrial base that had basically lain dormant for ten years, at a time when our nation had a population about one half of its present size and almost all able-bodied young men were in the military. "To American production," Soviet dictator Joseph Stalin toasted at the 1943 summit conference in Teheran, "without which this war would have been lost."

The glory and honor for our hard-won triumph belongs to our combat soldiers, sailors, marines, and airmen who fought with inspiring courage on a thousand battlefields and died by the hundreds of thousands. Carefully documented accounts of heroism challenge us to recognize their sacrifices and pay them homage. Some of the most notable acts of courage and sacrifice went unrecorded because there were no witnesses left alive to testify about them. What Admiral Chester Nimitz said of the performance of marines on Iwo Jima—"Uncommon valor was a common virtue"—could have been said justly of our soldiers, airmen, marines, and sailors all over the world.

But our fighters would not have prevailed were they not

supported by our vast industrial machine. The world had never seen industrial productivity on such a scale. The numbers still challenge the imagination. Prominent economists predicted that the end of the war would bring hard times when the government shut down war industries and millions of servicemen were set free looking for work. In Washington, our leaders fretted about a possible return to the despair of the 1930s. But instead we stepped immediately into a sustained economic expansion.

In retrospect, the boom that followed World War II seems merely logical. For the duration of the war, our industry had committed all of its effort to war production. For four years no cars, washing machines, toasters, radios, or other basic commodities rolled off the assembly lines. Thus, when peace broke out there was tremendous pent-up consumer demand.

Also, consumers were flush with cash. Millions of war production workers had been earning excellent wages. The pay of factory workers almost doubled during the war, but there was precious little to spend their newly found wealth on. What few goods were available could not be bought for money alone; you also had to have ration points, which were allotted by bureaucratic formula.

Thus, the moment war production ceased and wartime economic regulation was suspended, we bounded through a quick transformation into something new: a true consumer economy. Before long millions of ex-servicemen were working on assembly lines from coast to coast. The postwar baby boom stoked the economic furnace. We sailed into the 1950s amid robust demand and steadily expanding manufacturing industries. The rest of the world looked upon our economic performance in awe, and none were more envious than our communist competitors. In the 1950s, the Soviet Union beat us into space with the famous *Sputnik* but it never matched our interstate highway system or plethora of consumer products.

America the beautiful truly was America the bountiful, but victory and success can summon as many intractable problems as defeat and failure. The prosperity of the 1950s and 1960s bred smugness and complacency. As Germany and Japan rebuilt their industries, rising like the mythical phoenix from the ashes of war, we scarcely noticed. When they quietly began to export higher quality products to our shores, we were slow to react. A few lonely prophets of change, such as the great W. Edwards Deming, warned of a coming quality revolution, but they were voices crying in the wilderness.

By the 1970s, many of our major manufacturing industries were struggling to survive against seemingly invincible foreign competition. The oil embargos, which greatly enhanced the value and desirability of fuel-efficient foreign cars, underscored our vulnerability. Suddenly there was serious talk among knowledgeable people that American manufacturing could no longer compete with the industrial giants of Japan and Germany. The once mighty industrial complexes of middle America became a "rust belt" of shuttered factories and obsolete machinery. Economists and scholars solemnly intoned that Americans would have to learn to live with less as the torch of international leadership passed on to more vigorous nations. President Jimmy Carter seemed to give official sanction to that view in his infamous "malaise" speech.

About the same time we awoke as if from a dream to discover that many basic American values—honesty, patriotism, self-reliance, monogamy—were also under stress. The divisiveness of the Vietnam War accelerated an apparent breakdown in public morality as many of our young people "tuned in, turned on, and dropped out." Drug addiction cast an ominous shadow across the landscape. Likewise, many of our primary media of cultural expression—movies, novels, and television—descended into a vale of amoral opportunism from which they have yet to emerge. With minimal fanfare or preparation, we all became addicted to the revolutionary new power of television, which began to exercise profound and not universally appreciated influence on our lifestyles and values.

TV started low on the cultural food chain and went downhill. It is worth noting that the era in which Newton Minow, as chairman of the Federal Communications Commission, labeled television "a vast wasteland" is now known to us as "the golden age of television."

Of course, evidence of societal decline is always abundant and invariably exaggerated. *"O tempora! O mores!"* cried the ancient Roman orator Cicero, lamenting the perceived erosion of civic consciousness at a time when the Roman empire had hardly begun its eight-hundred-year lifespan and its greatest days lay in the future. We likewise have an alarmist tendency to overstate the pathologies we see about us.

"Disaster is rarely as pervasive as it seems from recorded accounts," wrote the late historian Barbara Tuchman in *A Distant Mirror.* "The fact of being on the record makes it appear continuous and ubiquitous whereas it is more likely to have been sporadic both in time and place. Besides, persistence of the normal is usually greater than the effect of disturbance, as we know from our own times. After absorbing the news of today, one expects to face a world consisting entirely of strikes, crimes, power failures, broken water mains, stalled trains, school shutdowns, muggers, drug addicts, neo-Nazis, and rapists. The fact is that one can come home in the evening—on a lucky day—without having encountered more than one or two of these phenomena."

Our images of our own lives are irrevocably distorted by perceptions transmitted and repeated by the media. For example, the summer of 1969 is commonly associated with the Woodstock rock festival in New York, where upward of four hundred thousand young people cavorted in the mud amid various forms of rowdiness and drug abuse. Our popular cul-

ture has established that event as the coming-of-age of the
"Woodstock generation," which, so the pundits assure us, was
some sort of turning point in American cultural evolution.

I retain a totally different recollection of the summer of
1969. I was a senior executive with NASA. We were embarked
upon one of the most visionary and exciting missions in the
history of our species—the Apollo moon shot. Thousands of
the people engaged in that great adventure were youngsters
fresh out of college. I remember them well. They were not
stoked up on drugs or rolling naked in the mud. They were
well dressed and extraordinarily well behaved. Most of all, they
were committed to what we were doing. They were working
incredible hours, sometimes around the clock, in working conditions that were often primitive. It was enough for them that
their country was embarked upon a historic quest, and they
were honored to be part of it. Their zeal and commitment
made it happen and it is they, not the Woodstock hippies, who
represented the future of this great nation.

Similarly, I regard the conflict in Vietnam not as a traumatic
collapse of American will but rather as an isolated defeat in a
fifty-year war that we eventually won. I share our national grief
for the young men who died in that desolate jungle and regret
they were ever sent there. But to the extent that we erred it
was in our choice of where and when to fight communism, not
in the cause itself, and even that issue is debatable. Our Vietnam struggle came at a time when communist China was trying to subvert other nations in Southeast Asia, notably
Indonesia and Singapore. Had we not fought in Vietnam,
those nations may well have succumbed to communism with
far-reaching repercussions for the entire world.

OUR LONG TWILIGHT STRUGGLE

The collapse of communism is a topic that astounds me not
because it finally happened but because of the blasé way we

reacted to it. For the better part of this century we were engaged in an intense ideological struggle with a movement that challenged our most basic principles. We dubbed it the cold war, though it certainly was not very cold to the young men who fought in Korea and Vietnam. For a time in the 1960s and 1970s, it seemed we were going to lose. Communist nations were springing up all over the world, and many democracies were beset by large and vigorous domestic communist movements.

Indeed, many of our own most influential intellectuals were adamant that capitalism was a dinosaur drawing its last dying breaths. That was only a few years ago, but my, how times have changed.

The appeal of communist dogma was easy to understand. It was born of the best of intentions in the minds of scholarly academics who were appalled by the economic inequity and oppression they saw around them. Within the communist vision, every worker was supposed to have a job, ample food, adequate housing, decent clothing, available medical care, and all of the basic amenities of life. That was why so many good people—many of them Americans—cherished hopes for the communist movement and overlooked the excesses committed on its behalf, even when those excesses explored the outer reaches of human depravity.

Nor can there be any question that the various communist regimes had more than sufficient power to translate their vision into reality. They had complete authority to imprison, exile, or shoot anyone who stood in their way, and they used that authority without compunction.

It was the same everywhere communism took root—Poland, East Germany, Hungary, Czechoslovakia, Romania, Bulgaria, Austria, Cuba, North Korea, North Vietnam, Albania, Yemen, Ethiopia, and Angola. If you had the misfortune to live there, you either signed on to the system or paid a dear price. Cooperation was assumed, participation was mandatory, and dissent was usually fatal. Yet despite the diversity of nations pursuing the communist vision, the unlimited power of their governments, the extensive cooperation among them during communism's heyday, and the active support of influential intellectuals in the West, the communist dream failed to achieve its goals anywhere. Instead, it suddenly and unexpectedly collapsed like a house of cards hit with a gust of wind.

Oliver Wendell Holmes Sr., father of the famous Supreme Court justice, wrote a popular poem called "The Deacon's Masterpiece" about a celebrated one-hoss shay (a horse-drawn buggy) that was built so well that no one part of it could wear out before any other. Eventually it disintegrated all at once, leaving its surprised driver sitting amid a pile of rubble. Holmes's poem was a satire on the severe strain of Puritanism that once dominated New England society and then suddenly faded. The precipitous collapse of communism was like Holmes's one-hoss shay. It just came apart all at once as if some great supernatural force decreed that this failed experiment had gone on long enough.

Now we are left to clean up the mess left in communism's wake—dilapidated housing, antiquated industry, chronic shortages of medicine, scarce consumer goods of lousy quality, and unprecedented environmental destruction.

The latter is perhaps the most visible of communism's legacies and underscores my contention that environmental protection is a function of a vigorous industrial economy. Where economic growth is stagnant and poverty is rampant there is little interest in environmental protection and scant resources to invest in it. The landscape of the former communist states is littered with cesspools of industrial effluent and haphazard mounds of toxic wastes carelessly dumped across the open countryside. The air in many places is befouled with incredible amounts of pollution emitted by factory smokestacks without scrubbers of any kind. Once bountiful rivers and lakes have been corrupted, seemingly beyond redemption.

I have said before that Mother Nature is a resilient lady, and so she is, but she will need all of her regenerative powers to atone for the ravages of central economic planning and unbridled good intentions.

From beginning to end there lay at the heart of communism a malignant cancer of tyranny whose claim to legitimacy was so conspicuously fraudulent that over time fewer and fewer citizens were able to believe in it, no matter how much they wanted to. It is the basic tenet of modern dictatorships that they aspire to serve the needs of most of their citizens, at least in terms of maintaining a viable economy and enabling people to go about their daily lives with minimal harassment. Where the dictatorship arises from social and economic chaos, which is invariably the case, there are always legions of people eager to believe in it and cooperate with it.

"Social democracy, far from conditioning the masses against one-man rule, encouraged them to accept if not seek it," wrote philosopher Robert Nisbet. "The horrifying record of torture, imprisonment, and mass execution that the dictators of this century, especially those on the political left, have left to posterity may easily obscure the fact that it was always minorities, not majorities, whom the Stalins and Hitlers imprisoned and exterminated. Everything is done by the tyrant in the modern world, as in the ancient, to keep the majority of people fed and protected."

But communism failed to achieve even that most primal requirement and thus is now a historical footnote awaiting the final demise of its last remaining outposts in Cuba, Vietnam, and North Korea. (China is rapidly embracing capitalism, though it continues to pay lip service to communist ideology. The Peking dictatorship is just another cabal of thugs clinging to power. Its days are numbered.) It is almost unbearable to contemplate the millions of lives sacrificed to the fraudulent communist vision, which from beginning to end was a vehicle for unbridled tyranny.

"In truth, many of us who supported the socialist bloc to the bitter end believed for a long time that the political Byzantinism, mass murders, and bureaucratic rigidities of socialism would be overcome," wrote Eugene D. Genovese in the April 17, 1995, issue of *The New Republic*. "We overestimated the weaknesses of capitalism and we underestimated the weaknesses of socialism. In effect, we remained convinced that capitalism could not solve its problems but that socialism would solve its own. But those latter problems were not passing, they were intrinsic. And so our blunder, as blunders go, was a beaut."

Of course, the collapse of communism did not just happen all on its own. Around the world a variety of critics, one of which was the U.S. Chamber of Commerce, worked doggedly over a period of many years to expose the defects of the marxist vision.

Most of our work centered around the endless struggle to influence this nation's political process and the rebutting of the leftist propaganda that inundated much of our society during the 1960s and 1970s. At times it seemed no one outside the *Reader's Digest* editorial staff was willing to defend our economic system.

In 1971, Justice Lewis Powell, several years before he was nominated to the Supreme Court, wrote a powerful memorandum to the U.S. Chamber of Commerce board of directors exhorting us to become more active in the national debate about social and economic principles. We took his message to heart and soon assumed a prominent place in the national debate, launching a variety of print and electronic media outreach campaigns.

Before long we broadened our efforts into the southern

hemisphere, where several nations were actively flirting with communism and falling under the influence of Soviet and Chinese propaganda. A steady stream of political and business leaders from Latin America were invited to visit our headquarters in Washington, where we encouraged them to help propagate the free enterprise faith. They were instrumental in establishing U.S.-style chambers of commerce throughout Central and South America, which are today powerful advocates of political and economic freedom. We were unstintingly generous with our time and resources, sharing our expertise with Latin American leaders who were then only beginning to understand and embrace the principles of free enterprise in their own countries.

When we began that campaign, virtually all of the nations of Latin America were repressive police states in which government planners wielded broad powers over their nation's economies. Today, only Cuba remains committed to that folly.

Our success in Latin America emboldened us to more daring efforts to actively propagate free enterprise values behind the Iron Curtain and challenge the reigning marxist orthodoxy. Our approach was not to lecture but to educate, not to attack communism directly but rather to celebrate the virtues and advantages of capitalism.

In 1980, I applied for permission to visit mainland China to lecture college students about capitalism. At the time it seemed rather far-fetched that the Chinese leaders in Peking would permit the head of the free world's largest business federation to preach an anticommunist message to their young people, but we kept after them and after much negotiating I finally wangled an invitation.

Upon my arrival, I was greatly disappointed to learn I was scheduled to speak not to students but to a sea of sad-sack communist bureaucrats all dressed alike in that dreary Mao uniform. It occurred to me then that the entire exercise might be a waste of time. I figured at the least I would beard the communist lion in his den and make a hasty getaway—perhaps with a real Peking duck or two under my arm.

But as fate would have it, the deputy director of planning for the communist party was in the hall and became intensely interested in what I had to say. Upon her insistence, I was invited back the next day to address a gathering of top bureaucrats from the planning administration about the importance of incentives in encouraging productivity.

Oddly, one of my most compelling memories of that first trip to China was not of the sumptuous banquets or endless toasts of government officials I was obliged to endure but of an encounter I had with a rather forlorn looking factory worker who spent his days fashioning artifacts of various kinds from coral. He told me, through an interpreter, of course, that he averaged two years' labor on each piece that he made. He had been assigned to that job straight out of high school forty years before by command of some communist bureaucrat, and there he was, still making those little artifacts.

In 1989, I returned to China and this time got my wish to speak to college students at the University of Peking. I had expected to be in a small lecture hall with a few well-chosen cadres, but instead I was in a hall designed for two hundred students that was jam-packed with about twelve hundred. They were sitting two to a seat, wedged tightly together on the floors, and crammed into windows and doorways.

All of those students understood English and were eager to learn about free enterprise. They recognized change was coming and wanted to be part of it. I felt the tension in the air that day, and the ground moving beneath my feet, a few weeks before the great demonstration in Tienenmen Square. The day before the lecture, I was invited to meet with Vice Premier Li Peng in the Great Hall of the People. A rumor was afoot that the communist leadership was about to reimpose economic controls upon the country. I warned Li Peng it would be a terrible mistake that would inevitably promote social disruption. He listened politely, but obviously he did not heed my advice.

The massacre at Tienenmen Square was a major setback to the progress of human freedom in China, but the cause is far from lost. Those who advocate repeal of China's most favored nation status fail to grasp how much substantive progress we have made in liberating more than one billion human beings. In China today ordinary citizens can make critical decisions about their personal futures without consulting bureaucrats. They can open stores, sell agricultural produce, launch new ventures, and change jobs. They do not yet have political freedom, but they enjoy great economic freedom, which is a precursor of political freedom. The same forces that transformed South America are at work today in China—driven by free enterprise.

Shortly after that second trip to China, I attended a social event at the Czechoslavakian embassy in Washington, where I was invited to visit Prague to discuss business and trade issues. The communist bloc still loomed across the world landscape like a mighty colossus in those days, powerful and intimidating. There was as yet no whisper of the great changes just over the horizon.

I accepted the invitation on condition that I be permitted to lecture on capitalism, free markets, and freedom of the press and that my audience include businesspeople and college students. My hosts readily agreed to these conditions.

It was a replay of my experience in Peking. When I spoke to students at the University of Prague, it was standing room only for the first speech celebrating economic and political freedom given there in forty years. The air seemed electric as those young people asked me question after question about our system and demanded to know when the celebrated perestroika then appearing in the Soviet Union would reach Prague. I exhorted them not to wait but to take their future into their own hands.

The striking thing to me was their fascination with economic opportunity. To be sure, they felt keenly their lack of political freedom, the basic human rights to express their own views and peacefully remove government officials, but that was old news to them. They had only recently begun to think about economic freedom and to realize that economic and political freedom are two sides of the same coin: that you cannot long have one without the other. In the end it was the craving for economic freedom and opportunity that destroyed communism—the very same craving that had given birth to the marxist vision so many years before.

THE WORLD AS WE MAKE IT

Now that our longtime communist rival has bitten the dust and tacitly acknowledged the superiority of political and economic freedom, we are neither relieved nor thrilled but merely obsessed with our own perceived shortcomings and defects. Such dreariness of spirit does not become us, honor our heritage, or augur well for the future.

It has become a commonplace to compare unrelated failures to the success of the Apollo moon mission. We often hear someone say, "We can put men on the moon, but we can't deliver mail across town," or, "We can put men on the moon, but we cannot do anything about AIDS."

The key difference, of course, is that putting men on the moon required a concentrated effort by a group of highly motivated people to solve what was basically a technical challenge. But moving mail and preventing communicable diseases like AIDS involves persuading ordinary people to accept responsibility, observe high standards, and behave reasonably. Compared to that, putting men on the moon was a breeze.

We got off on the wrong foot a long time ago when we substituted legalisms for individual judgment and began trying to specify precise limits and requirements for a wide range of human activities that simply will not yield to such tidy organization. Over the years we have accumulated literally tens of thousands of pages of laws, rules, and regulations in a fruitless endeavor to legislate our way to the promised land. It cannot be done because it does not speak to the heart of the human dilemma. There is only one law of consequence—that we should treat other people the way we expect them to treat us. Everything else is commentary.

In the 1930s, millions of Americans did not have enough to eat, much less the panoply of technological wizardry that today graces most homes, even in poor neighborhoods. But the crime rates of the 1930s were a tiny fraction of what they are today, and millions of homes—at least those in small towns and rural areas—didn't even have locks on the doors. As recently as the 1960s this was true in many parts of the country.

It is simply not rational to attribute our soaring crime rates to poverty. Morality is not a financial commodity; it is an expression of values. Nor is it rational to blame racism or sexism or any other ism for the crumbling social fabric we see in tatters all about us. Prejudice and discrimination surely still exist but clearly are less a factor in life than they were a generation ago when our streets were relatively safe and most of our families intact. There are other forces at work undermining our social cohesiveness and they permeate all of society, not just the bottom rungs. To be effective, any coherent plan to turn things around must begin with society's elite.

"The law, in all its majestic equality," wrote Anatole France, "forbids the rich as well as the poor to sleep under bridges, to beg in the streets, and to steal bread." Newspapers and business journals are filled to overflowing with accounts of misdeeds and appalling behavior in high places. In recent years we have even seen prominent ministers defrocked and hauled off to jail for financial and sexual misconduct. Political leaders at times seem oblivious to any sense of right and wrong. Frequent headlines detail corruption and abuse of power by police. Corporate leaders all too often fail to adhere to high moral and ethical standards.

Any attempt to reestablish social norms must begin with the elite and then be embraced by the middle class. Then and only then will we have the moral standing to lecture people at the bottom of the ladder.

Business bears a solemn responsibility to set examples of honesty and civic responsibility. The integrity of an organization must begin with the top leadership. If the top people are looting their expense accounts, deceiving the directors, and abusing subordinates, that attitude will be reflected throughout the organization. If integrity does not begin at the top, there is little chance of it beginning anywhere.

Similarly, any attempt to get this nation back on a more solid moral footing must include prominent figures in academia, the arts, and public service. It steams me to turn on the television and see celebrities whose personal lifestyles would embarrass a goat lecture the rest of us about our allegedly stingy policies toward the poor. The primary cause of poverty in this country today is family breakdown caused by aimless young men and women conceiving children out of wedlock. No government program can rectify that disaster, but it would help a lot if prominent celebrities set moral examples for those clueless kids having illegitimate babies to notice and emulate. Former vice president Dan Quayle's potshot at *Murphy Brown* for glamorizing out-of-wedlock motherhood was right on the money. He initially took a lot of heat for that criticism, but before long some of his most outspoken critics were grudgingly admitting he had a valid point.

It has become unfashionable to pass critical judgment on forms of behavior that would have been roundly condemned a generation ago. To the extent that our society refrains from condemning destructive, irresponsible, and immoral conduct, it cannot expect people to restrain their more basic impulses.

Believe it or not, there really is an overwhelming consensus among Democrats and Republicans, liberals and conservatives, blacks and whites, men and women, elderly people and young people that our society desperately needs recognizable limits on human behavior that we can all rally around and help reinforce. We cannot regulate offensive behavior as such, except when it violates the law, but we can bring back the social opprobrium—the *shame*—once associated with antisocial activities. Shame is a powerful force in human relations and one that most people will respond to.

THE NEW MILLENNIUM

We have established to the world's satisfaction that the greatest hope for mankind lies within our vision of a system that honors political and economic freedom, leaving individual citizens to pursue their own dreams and succeed or fail according to their own fortunes. This was no small achievement and we owe it to ourselves to ponder our victory, consider its implications, and document it carefully for the edification of future generations.

We have suffered some wounds and losses along the way, but we have emerged intact. Despite the conspicuous scandals and lurid headlines, the great majority of Americans go about their business with time-honored respect for the eternal verities. The values that sustained us through the Great Depression and World War II are still in evidence as an integral part of the

American character. They are visible in a million vital ways in our daily life. Most business executives rise early and work late, striving to achieve high standards of excellence. Most contracts are honored and most personal pledges are kept. More than a hundred million workers ply their trades and crafts daily at a remarkably high level of skill and commitment. Most of our citizens demonstrate high moral character and civic responsibility. The great majority of our young people do *not* abuse illegal drugs or conceive illegitimate children.

Similarly, our commerce and industry are today setting records in efficiency and productivity that would have been unimaginable even a few years ago. We were late to recognize the quality challenge of foreign competition, but when we did we rose to meet it and are today teaching the Japanese and Germans a thing or two.

Most important for our economic future, we have reasserted our world leadership at the cutting edge of the technological revolution—in microprocessing, biotechnology, electronics, software, aeronautics, pharmaceuticals, medical research, and engineering. We are again the world's largest exporter in terms of dollar value of exports. Our industrial base is humming like a three-penny finishing nail hit with a greasy ball peen hammer.

In a time when progress is racing ahead at breakneck speed, our creativity and flexibility stand us in good stead. According to the Council on Competitiveness, our growth rates in standard of living, manufacturing productivity, and investment in plant and equipment in 1994 were the highest in a decade. In 1995, for the second year in a row, the World Economic Forum and the International Institute for Management Development ranked the United States number one as the world's most competitive economy. Japan, which headed the survey from 1986 through 1993, had fallen to fourth place by 1995. Clearly we are doing something right.

We have our problems, as does every nation, but we have a vast reservoir of national character, cultural cohesion, and intellectual resources to draw upon as we approach the millennium and prepare to embark upon the twenty-first century. The challenges before us are serious but by no means overwhelming. The major impediments we must overcome are the false imagery and self-deception that still cloud our intellectual discourse and political debates and an entrenched big government mentality out of step with the modern age.

I remain at heart an optimist. I cannot believe we have come this far only to succumb to self-delusion, bureaucratic inertia, and fiscal irresponsibility. As the century nears its end and a new millennium hovers on the horizon, we enjoy an extraordinary abundance of advantages and opportunities such as empower no other nation. Our material wealth, despite our continuing impecuniousness, remains vast and sufficient to our most ambitious undertakings. Our national security, in the wake of communism's collapse, is virtually immune to serious threat (at least until Iran gets its hands on nuclear weapons). Our people retain an extraordinary level of the basic civic virtues that are the foundation of any great nation and only wait to be summoned to action by inspired leadership.

Amid the daily hassles, nit-picking, and infighting of daily life, there are visionary people calling us to higher things. We cannot hear because we're too busy yelling at each other. We cannot see because we refuse to give up our illusions. We cannot act because we are not unified.

The small business community stood up and made a difference in 1994. A big difference. The power it displayed was awesome and has tremendous potential to achieve great things. But the speed of a runaway horse counts for nothing, and the power of small business will simply sputter out if it is not focused on clear and attainable objectives.

We dare not let that happen. The vision of the small business revolution is clear and enjoys broad public support. Its basic elements are a smaller, less intrusive federal government that works with small business instead of against it; that regulates only when necessary and then at the least possible cost; that is managed with common sense; that is more concerned about productive investment than about consumption; that permits the greatest possible leeway for personal freedom and initiative; that stresses responsibilities as much as rights; that respects traditional societal and family values; and that lives within its finances.

Chambers of commerce at the federal, state, and local level offer the best and most effective mechanism for harnessing the power of small business and making certain it is a power for good. Working together at the local, state, and national level, we can coordinate the small business revolution and make certain its latent power is fully brought to bear on our most vexing challenges.

We do not need an external threat to force us to put aside our petty differences and grievances and work together. I speak as one who helped put men on the moon and who knows what is possible. In the present crisis, even a modest reckoning with reality will take us a long way.

EPILOGUE

The small business revolution of 1994 was only a beginning and has a long way to go before it can be considered an accomplished fact. In a democracy, the most difficult task is to take away freebies from citizens who have become accustomed to them. It is equally difficult for political leaders to make painful choices between abstract degrees of safety promised to consumers and workers by regulations and the costs of those regulations imposed upon private business. Both areas lend themselves to political demagoguery, which is currently flying fast and furiously along the corridors of Congress and out into the airwaves and newsprint of the nation. A perfectly sensible and long overdue proposal to save Medicare from bankruptcy is branded an attack on senior citizens. An increase of 5.5 percent in funding for school lunches is labeled a "cut" by the vice president of the United States. Efforts to impose fiscal sanity on environmental regulation are greeted with carefully orchestrated hysteria. Legislation to transform OSHA into a useful provider of information and consultation, backed by enforcement power when it is needed, is denounced as a betrayal of working people. And so forth and so on. In the face of unremitting assault, some lukewarm allies of the small business revolution are getting cold feet. Many of these are longtime members of Congress who are hedging their bets, waiting to see if the small business revolution has staying power or will fade away with the next electoral cycle.

I believe the small business revolution is here to stay and

will have a decisive influence on our political process for many years to come. The American people want government off their backs. The experts and insiders can manipulate poll questions and answers to support their biases, and "trends" in public opinion are as malleable as the wind, but election results carry the day.

To their everlasting credit, the small business stalwarts who came off the sidelines in 1994 to assert leadership in Congress have not wavered from their commitment or yielded to the threats of demagoguery. Together with their families and employees, they represent what's best in America and our best hope for reasserting the traditional values of honesty, hard work, and investment in the future that made this country great and keep it in the forefront of the world's nations. In the present crisis, it is up to business—and especially small business—to redouble our efforts to elect and reelect probusiness candidates across the board until the small business revolution is a done deal and our government is once again a credible force in American life.

AUTHOR'S NOTE ON
SOURCES

❖

The facts, quotes, insights, anecdotes, and other information in this book were derived from a variety of sources, including government agencies, newspapers, magazines, and Washington think tanks, where droves of earnest policy analysts produce a steady stream of position papers on just about every social, political, and economic issue that comes before our government. The quotes from members of Congress and executives of state and local chambers of commerce were derived from personal interviews or written responses to queries.

Among the federal agencies whose official reports and publications are cited herein are the Office of Management and Budget, Congressional Budget Office, Congressional Research Service, Library of Congress, Bureau of Labor Statistics, Environmental Protection Agency, Occupational Safety and Health Administration, Food and Drug Administration, and Office of Personnel Management.

The think tanks whose various publications and reports provided useful background for this work include The Heritage Foundation, Cato Institute, Citizens for a Sound Economy, Reason Foundation, American Enterprise Institute, Center for the Study of American Business, The Lincoln Institute, Employment Policies Institute, and Family Research Council.

Newspaper sources include the *Washington Post, Washington Times, New York Times, Wall Street Journal, Investors' Business Daily, Detroit News, Wichita Business Journal,* and *Legal Times.* Magazine sources include *U.S. News & World Report, Washington Monthly, Insight, Fortune, Regulation, American Spectator, Time, Newsweek, Science, National Review, New Republic,* and *Forbes.*

The following are individuals listed in alphabetical order whose news reports, editorials, and anecdotes are cited or provided a basis for commentary:

Adler, Jonathan H. "Taking Cause," *National Review,* December 19, 1994.

Alter, Dr. Harvey. "Everybody Wants Clean Air," *Environmental Science and Technology,* September 1987.

Ames, Bruce. "Dietary Carcinogens and Anti-Carcinogens," *Science,* September 1983.

Angel, Marcia. "Are Breast Implants Actually OK?" *The New Republic,* September 11, 1995.

Bailey, Jeff. "Curbside Recycling Comforts the Soul, but Benefits Are Scant," *Wall Street Journal,* January 19, 1995.

Barrett, Paul M. "Supreme Court Prepares to Decide If Regulators Have Gone Too Far to Aid Endangered Species," *Wall Street Journal,* April 14, 1995.

Bennett, Michael J. *The Asbestos Racket,* Free Enterprise Press, 1991.

Berry, John M. "The Economy's Surprise: More High Wage Jobs," *Washington Post,* September 2, 1994.

Bolch, Bob and Howard Lyons. *Apocalypse Not,* Cato Institute, 1993.

Bowers, Brent. "FDA Regulatory Tide Swallows Up McCurdy Fish Company," *Wall Street Journal,* May 18, 1993.

Brought, Wayne T. *A Citizen's Guide to Making Sense Out of Regulation with Risk Assessment,* Citizens for a Sound Economy, 1995.

Budiansky, Stephen, with Ted Gest and David Fischer. "Are Lawyers Above the Law?" *U.S. News & World Report,* January 9, 1995.

Carey, Peter. "The Asbestos Panic Attack," *U.S. News & World Report,* February 20, 1995.

Carter, Hodding. "Alar Scare: A Case Study in Media's Skewed Reality," *Wall Street Journal,* April 20, 1989.

Causey, Mike. "Feds Need New Threads," *Washington Post,* February 19, 1985.

Charles, Robert B. "From Democracy to Regulocracy," *The World & I,* July 1995.

Crews, Clyde Wayne, Jr. "Ten Thousand Commandments: Regulatory Trends 1981–92 and the Prospects for Reform," *Journal of Regulation and Social Costs,* March 1993.

DeMuth, Christopher C. "The White House Review Programs," *Regulation,* January–February 1980.

Diaz, Tom. "Workers' Image Reflects Reality," *Washington Times,* April 5, 1983.

Dole, Senator Robert. "There's No Law Against Common Sense," *Washington Post,* March 5, 1995.

Easterbrook, Gregg. "Everything You Know About the Environment Is Wrong," *The New Republic,* April 30, 1990.

————. "The Spotted Owl: An Environmental Parable," *The New Republic,* March 28, 1994.

————. "Beyond Politics As Usual," *Washington Post Magazine,* April 9, 1995.

————. *A Moment on Earth: The Coming Age of Environmental Optimism,* Viking Press, 1995.

Eckerly, Susan M. *A Citizens Guide to Regulation,* The Heritage Foundation, 1994.

Fulco, Nancy, and David Voight. "Small Business and Regulation," U.S. Chamber of Commerce, February 14, 1995.

Gladwell, Malcolm. "Some Fear Bad Precedent in Alar Alarm," *Washington Post,* April 19, 1989.

Glassman, James K. "Another Galloping Entitlement," *Washington Post,* May 9, 1995.

Gugliotta, Guy. "Scaling Down the American Dream," *Washington Post,* April 19, 1995.

Harwood, Richard. "Corrections and the Beast," *Washington Post,* December 29, 1991.

Havender, William. "Politicians Make Bad Scientists," *Journal on Government and Society,* American Enterprise Institute, November–December 1981.

Hopkins, Thomas D. *Costs of Regulation: Filling the Gaps,* report for Regulatory Information Service Center, August 1992.

————. *The Costs of Federal Regulation,* National Chamber Foundation, 1992.

Horowitz, Sari. "D.C. School Board Draws Fire," *Washington Post,* March 23, 1995.

Judge, Clark. "Thresholds of Pain," *Wall Street Journal,* August 10, 1994.

Kenworthy, Tom. "GOP Plan to Broaden Property Rights Could Cost Public Dearly," *Washington Post,* March 13, 1994.

Krauthammer, Charles. "Dodging and Weaving on Affirmative Action," *Washington Post,* March 3, 1995.

————. "Vaccines for Children: Preview of Clintoncare," *Washington Post,* July 29, 1995.

————. "Counting by Race," *Washington Post,* September 1, 1995.

Lee, Gary. "Superseding Federal Safety Rules," *Washington Post,* February 10, 1995.

Lunner, Chet. "Government Spends Five Years to Study Five-Gallon Buckets," Gannett News Service, May 11, 1994.

Marshall, Jennifer E. "Sanctioning Illegitimacy: Our National Character Is at Stake," Family Research Council, 1995.

Mayer, Caroline E. "Getting Personal on Product Liability," *Washington Post,* March 7, 1995.

Merski, Paul G. "Minimum Wage Hike: A New $8 Billion Tax on Jobs," Citizens for a Sound Economy, January 31, 1995.

Mossman, B. T., J. Bignon, M. Corn, A. Seaton, and J. B. L. Gee. "Asbestos: Scientific Developments and Implications for Public Policy," *Science,* January 19, 1990.

Novak, Janet. "Ergopolitics 101," *Forbes,* October 24, 1994.

Pechman, Louis. "A Level Playing Field or a Quagmire?" *New York Times,* July 30, 1995.

Peters, Charles. "The Myth of the Underpaid Federal Worker," *Washington Post,* March 3, 1983.

Postrel, Virginia I. "How Bureaucratic Decrees Fuel the Nation's Rage," *Washington Post,* February 5, 1995.

Raspberry, William. "When Rules Collide with Common Sense," *Washington Post,* August 17, 1992.

————. "Strain on Our Civil Society," *Washington Post,* October 2, 1995.

Rector, Robert. "Poorly Understood Poverty," *American Enterprise,* January–February 1995.

Roberts, Leslie. "Costs of a Clean Environment," *Science,* March 8, 1991.

Samuelson, Robert J. "Unspeakable Runaway Spending," *Washington Post,* August 3, 1994.

————. "A Nation in Denial," *Newsweek,* March 8, 1995.

Schneider, Keith. "New View Calls Environmental Policy Misguided," *New York Times,* March 21, 1993.

Scroggin, Don G. "Study May Be Used to Challenge Environmental Regulations," *Legal Times,* October 3, 1983.

Shapiro, Joseph P., and Jennifer Seter. "Welfare: The Myth of Reform," *U.S. News & World Report,* January 16, 1995.

Singer, Fred S. "Fact and Fancy on Greenhouse Earth," *Wall Street Journal,* August 30, 1988.

Snow, Tony. "Deadly Political Symptoms," *Washington Times,* February 21, 1995.

Solomon, Caleb. "Study of Refinery Proves an Eye-Opener," *Wall Street Journal,* March 29, 1993.

Sowell, Thomas. "Social Merit Badges," *Washington Times,* February 21, 1995.

Sparrow, H.G. "EcoQuiz II: How Environmentally Correct Can You Get?" *Washington Post,* June 5, 1994.

Stanfield, Rochelle L. "Rutsville," *National Journal,* December 3, 1994.

Steele, Shelby. "Affirmative Action Must Go," *New York Times,* March 1, 1995.

Stigler, George. "The Government of the Economy," *Principles of Macroeconomics,* University of Pennsylvania, 1963.

Sugg, Ike C. "If a Grizzly Attacks, Drop Your Gun," *Wall Street Journal,* June 23, 1993.

Suplee, Curt. "Assessing the Risk in Contract's 'Cost-Benefit' Curb on Regulators," *Washington Post,* February 28, 1995.

Thompson, Dick. "Congressional Chain Saw Massacre," *Time,* February 27, 1995.

Tierney, John. "Not to Worry," *Hippocrates,* January–February 1988.

Tolman, Jonathan. *Of Mice and Men: A Look at the Endangered Species Act,* Citizens for a Sound Economy, November 30, 1994.

Torry, Saundra. "Just Your Average $137,900-a-Year Attorney," *Washington Post,* April 3, 1995.

Tottie, John S. *Entitlement Spending: Government Estimates vs. Reality,* Citizens for a Sound Economy, January 25, 1994.

Tucker, William. "Is Nature Too Good For Us?" *Harper's,* March 1982.

Uman, Myron F. editor, "Keeping Pace with Science and Engineering: Case Studies in Environmental Regulation," National Academy Press, 1993.

Voight, David. "The Future of American Business," U.S. Chamber of Commerce, January 1994.

Warren, Melinda. *Reforming the Federal Regulatory Process: Rhetoric or Reality?* Occasional Paper 138, Center for the Study of American Business, June 1994.

Will, George. "Davis-Bacon and the Wages of Racism," *Washington Post,* February 5, 1995.